POWER AND CONTROL

Escape From Violence

Donald W. Tiffany
Phyllis G. Tiffany

University Press of America,® Inc.
Lanham • New York • Oxford

University Press of America,® Inc.
4720 Boston Way
Lanham, Maryland 20706

12 Hid's Copse Rd.
Cumnor Hill, Oxford OX2 9JJ

Printed in the United States of America
British Library Cataloging in Publication Information Available

Library of Congress Cataloging-in-Publication Data

Tiffany, Donald W.
Power and Control : escape from violence / Donald W. Tiffany, Phyllis G. Tiffany.
p. cm.
Includes bibliographical references and index.
1. Violence—Psychological aspects. 2. Control (Psychology) 3. Self-efficacy. I. Tiffany, Phyllis G. II. Title.
RC569.5.V55T53 1999 153.8—dc21 99-048930 CIP

ISBN 0-7618-1553-8 (cloth: alk. ppr.)
ISBN 0-7618-1554-6 (pbk: alk. ppr.)

™ The paper used in this publication meets the minimum requirements of American National Standard for Information Sciences—Permanence of Paper for Printed Library Materials, ANSI Z39.48—1984

CONTENTS

CONTENTS

Figures

FOREWORD

Violence is a constant theme in our society. We are inundated with media reports of all kinds of violence. Stories of victimization, terrorism, mass murders, serial killers, and gang violence are unsettling topics generating enormous curiosity. In some cases, the face of someone arrested for a violent act typifies violence, in other instances the violence is anonymous and may even span decades, such as the investigation of the Unibomber. Because of this focus on violence, we feel vulnerable, at risk, and some feel afraid.

Perhaps the question asked most about violence in our society is, "Why?" Shootings in schools seem to have replaced our temporary interest in gang violence and the nihilistic killing of the past decade. The media directs our attention to the extraordinary stories, and then the eventual local angle implying the most grotesque events are about to happen in one's hometown. The movie industry capitalizes on violent action films, and television serves up a seemingly steady stream of violent fare disguised as drama, sports, or cartoons. The result is a spectacle of people blaming others and espousing theories in futile attempts to explain violence.

How do we make sense of these violent times? Moreover, and perhaps more importantly, is there anything that can be done to find common causes and help reduce the incidents of violence. One clear starting point is to recognize that violence begins with the behavior of individuals. Moreover, focusing on individual behavior and accountability is essential to a civilized society.

POWER AND CONTROL

In "Power and Control: Escape From Violence," Drs. Donald and Phyllis Tiffany offer an intellectual framework in which to help identify and understand the concept of individual control. As the authors note in their text, the goal of understanding is to identify an individual's strengths and weaknesses in ways to offer an individual's alternatives to anger and violence. The emphasis on individual responsibility and choice will be of value to readers who are looking for answers to the ways we think about and react to violence.

The future of our society will be based on an increasingly diverse population, living in an increasingly complex social construct. Violence may be a prominent feature of such a society. However, we would all prefer to live in a decent and civilized environment, and we need to know more about influencing individual behavior, power, and control. A better knowledge of the causes of violence may help us construct a better future. This book is a step toward that understanding.

W. Ronald Olin, Ph.D.
Chief of Police
Lawrence, Kansas

ACKNOWLEDGEMENTS

Thirty plus years of research does not happen without the dedication and assistance of many people. Our first and most heartfelt appreciation goes to the thousands of clients, patients and students that, through their sufferings and involvement, in one way or the other, provided most of the ideas that culminated in this volume. Many discussions, classes, and research projects contributed to the body of research and expanded our ideas beyond our single abilities.

Many professors and friends, such as Drs. Franklin C. Shontz, M. Erik and Beatrice Wright, Fritz Heider, Martin Scheerer, Francis D. Horowitz, Robert P. Markley, Thomas T. Jackson, Cameron J. Camp, Richard L. Schiefelbusch, Edward L. Wike, and Robert a. Dentler, gave immeasurable support and encouragement. For this, we are eternally grateful. Several students, most notably, Mike Foley, Nadine Leiker, Kay Dey and Rich Elder, pursued research projects that added much to our thinking, to our data base, and most importantly to our own confidence and enthusiasm about our work throughout the years. Lastly, we want to thank Allen Tiffany, Adeliza Lazzo-Diaz, and Karen Tiffany. Their writing suggestions and helpful ideas (many of which were given at the dinner table, some very early in their lives), pointed up their feelings and struggles for control in their ever expanding young worlds. These insights propelled us closer to our "sense of control" by convincing us our theory and research were moving closer to understanding and explaining the purpose of responsible control in our lives.

INTRODUCTION

In 1513, Miccolo Machiavelli wrote in THE PRINCE that, "Our freewill may not be altogether extinguished, I think it may be true that fortune is the ruler of half our actions, but that she allows the other half or thereabouts to be governed by us." Over 486 years ago, it was recognized that "fortune" or other factors outside our reach contributed to our loss of control – whether through our own internal conflicts or environmental pressures.

Our question is, "Do we have the resources to counteract these forces and pressures and, if so, how and how much?" After all of these years since THE PRINCE was printed, do we know how much "fortune is the ruler of half our actions"? Alternatively, do we know how much we are able to control or is "governed by us"? Do we know under what conditions or situations that we have the most or least control? Is it possible to increase our ability to control our environment and ourselves? Are we any better off than Machiavelli saw us to be nearly five centuries ago? Machiavelli appears to be saying that we govern half our actions, and fate, chance, and powerful others govern the other half, essentially leaving us with no control when you pit one against the other. We believe we have more control than that. How else can you explain all of human nature's accomplishments over the last several centuries.

Our thesis is that we are more Self-Directed than NonSelf-Directed. This difference varies by different personalities and different situations. These points are discussed in detail in the later chapters of the book.

In contrast to Machiavelli, William Ernest Henley's (1849-1903) poem INVICTUS tells us how he was able to shape his perceptions, experiences, and role in steadfastly maintaining control of his fate, even in the worse situations.

POWER AND CONTROL

INVICTUS

Our of the night that covers me,
Black as the Pit from pole to pole
I thank whatever Gods may be
For my unconquerable soul.

In the fell clutch of circumstance
I have not winced nor cried aloud.
Under the bludgeonings of chance
My head is bloody, but unbowed.

Beyond this place of wrath and tears
Looms but the Horror of the shade,
And yet the menace of the years
Finds, and shall find, me unafraid.

It matters not how strait the gate,
How charged with punishments the scroll,
I am the master of my fate:
I am the captain of my soul."

Our research in the area of "Power and Control: Escape from Violence" began more than thirty years ago when we discovered support for our interest in studying the experience of control in children. It was simply this: **The control we experience over ourselves or over the world around us is the most important cause of how we behave and live our lives *and* it is fundamental to good mental health.** Experienced Control Theory is a Four-Factor Model for understanding the way we feel about the events that direct our lives. A great deal of our research has uncovered the way control influences our lives generally and varies as a function of different situations. Many of our ideas, though compatible with theories of personality, go beyond these personality theories to emphasize the comprehensive aspects of control that are most salient in our day-to-day activities. *Problems with control underlie every psychological problem or psychiatric diagnosis*. Personal problems related to loss of control are highlighted throughout the book.

Clearly, we cannot control everything in our lives, nor should we try. Our understanding of control has changed as we have come to comprehend better the sources of control and learn how to deal with them. "Power and Control: Escape from Violence," provides a balanced and non-value-laden understanding of control within the context of empirically tested theory. The book explains how each of us strives for responsible balance of the controls that impinge on our lives. Our goal is to help each individual learn to develop a healthy approach for looking at the obstacles that life puts in our path each day, sorting out those that are worth keeping and those that are better disregarded. It is not our intent to prescribe a program for everyone's use. We cannot do that in this media. One size does not fit all. Specific programs must fit specific systems, organizations, or situations. It is important that the reader learns more about the world we live in, and recognize and understand the effects of different kinds and levels of control. Armed with such knowledge you will understand the people around you, and their control concerns and how they interact with yours.

We had three main concerns for writing "Power and Control: Escape from Violence." **First**, we define and explain the Four-Factor Model of Control and its relationship to your life. This includes the primary concerns for each individual regarding the balance of different control sources or components of control. Our interest is to emphasize the need to balance all the various controls in your life and to point out that these change constantly. It is also our intent to offer a practical measure of common sense for each reader. We identify selected control problems and the impact of particular situations on our experience of control. We also show how each individual may responsibly take charge of his or her life. Our thesis is, "*If we have a normal amount of responsible control, we would commit no violence.*"

Second, our theory is based on research, but research that can tolerate common sense interpretation or practical understanding of day-to-day behavior. Our earliest investigations were directed primarily at assessing preadolescents – ages' eight to twelve. We found that it was possible to determine reliably how much they felt in control of their lives. Further, we were able to demonstrate that emotionally disturbed children experienced significantly more control from their parents than children who were not emotionally disturbed. The most important research finding came later, and quite by accident. We were interested in how experienced control effected creativity. We simply proposed that the more control a child experienced over his or her environment, the more creative he or she would be. Our hypothesis proved correct. Children who did not experience control over their situations did not demonstrate creativity in the task, but they exhibited another unexpected characteristic. They had a morbid fear of death. They feared separation from their families, feared being lost, and were sure they would die! The link between fear of death and an experienced loss of control suggested the profound importance of understanding the role 'loss of control' plays across the life span, which starts very early.

We launched a programmatic study to probe this frontier with adults as well as children. Our team effort, combining a clinical practice with an academic setting, enabled us to both generate and test ideas regarding observations about the way individuals attempt to control or react to the lack of control in their lives.

Control Theory represents the continuous evolution of our research in understanding control problems, whether they are individual or international. As graduate students in the early 1960's, Dr. M. Erik Wright told us that we had at least 30 years of work on Control Theory ahead of us. We think he was optimistic and feel we still have a long way to go to understand fully the impact of control on "our actions." Our development of the computerized test, the Tiffany Control Scales is an attempt in that direction.

Third, our intent is to provide you with better *tools* to help you learn to balance the controls in your life. Around your house, you have many books and manuals on how to operate or run household appliances. How to operate or 'run' your children or yourself is often taken for granted. We offer "Power and Control: Escape from Violence" as a manual toward better human understanding, from individuals to nations. The book teaches you how to cope with the most basic of problems, i.e., how to maintain control of yourself, your environment, and perhaps the world you touch or that touches you!

To the mental health professional, we offer the Experienced Control Model as a means of integrating clinical work with the Tiffany Control Scales. The ideas presented here do not tie you to a single theoretical approach. We heed the classic warning of Abraham H. Maslow, who cautioned us in 1966 against the commitment to a single treatment orientation. He stated, "If the only tool you have is a hammer (you tend) to treat everything as if it were a nail". Control Theory provides a shop with many tools, not just a hammer. With the tools provided, many different types of programs could be developed to help alter control problems, such as in schools, work places, national policy, etc. Our philosophy is to solve the small problems first (develop tools) so the bigger problems (programs for anger and violence) do not look so big.

We live in a world that is on a collision course between the sterile, impersonal, and mechanistic behavior of running such things as computers ***and*** the increasing need for effective self and interpersonal understanding. Such opposing forces can only result in internal and external conflict for the individual who lacks an understanding of how to control his/her own life. "Power and Control: Escape from Violence" will further enlighten the understanding of control problems, and hence, all problems, by providing each individual with the tools for becoming more in control of life situations.

Donald W. Tiffany, Ph.D., FAClinP
Phyllis G. Tiffany, Ph.D.

Chapter 1: Experiencing Control

A respected bank executive sets his clock to awaken at four AM to kill a girlfriend because he saw her with another man. An established minister sees his children off to school in the morning, locks his wife in the bedroom, and rapes her. A female business manager of a medium size store is afraid to wander off the well-worn path from her home to her job and becomes extremely hostile if forced to deviate from her customary route. A very religious teen-age female periodically blacks out and no organic cause can be found – even using the MRI. A middle-aged woman incurs frequent migraines and the MRI and other medical tests were negative for any neurological problems. Gang members' stab and kill other gang members at a social party for no apparent reason. Young parents kill their children as though their deaths were meaningless. School children shoot their playmates and even their teachers because they were not 'group members.' Workers shoot peers in the workplace without regard for the loss of human life and at costs estimated to be in the billions. On and on it goes with violence getting worst in style (Jeffrey Dohmer), frequency (Ted Bundy), magnitude (Timothy McVeigh), reason (Mark O. Barton) and place (schoolyard killings).

In 1997, the American Psychological Society released a Human Capital Initiative on Reducing Violence.[1] This initiative recognizes that "violence is a public health problem as perilous as any disease." In addition, it adds that "Simply punishing violent offenders, whether juveniles or adults, is not as reasonable as it sounds if the goal is to prevent future violence." More simply, violence begets violence.

All this in the face of national statistics showing stability or declining serious crime rates. Nonetheless, "today one in every 10,000 people will become the victim of homicide, a rate that has doubled since WWII." In addition, "nearly three in every 10,000 young males will be murdered. Among minority males between the ages of 16 and

25 who live in impoverished areas of large cities, the rate is more than 10 times higher – one in every 333," (see footnote #1).

Research of the PsycINFO database of the American Psychological Association shows the trend in studies regarding 'power.' Searching a database of 1,065,577 records published since 1887, we found the following number of references to power. Clearly, the 27 references to power in the period of 1887 to 1899 is a far cry from the 17,197 references to power in the period of 1976 to 1998. These numbers obviously signify that the concept of power has increasingly become a focus of social-psychological research over the last 111 years. These totals are not adjusted for the increased number of social scientists during this same period. It is interesting that the lowest percent of 'power' publications were published following WWII, making it clear that the number of studies is more a reflection of the times than a growth in the number of scientists.

YEAR	NO.	INCREASE
1887-1899	27	0
1900-1925	217	88%
1926-1950	1904	89%
1951-1975	4459	57%
1976-1998	17197	74%

If we examine the 'power' references over the last seven years, we find the following. There were 813 references for 1990, 885 for 1991 (increased 8%), 932 for 1992 (increased 5%), 1036 for 1993 (increased 10%), 1084 for 1994 (increased 4%), 1032 for 1995 (decreased 5%), 1020 for 1996 (decreased 1%) and 1070 for 1997 (increased 5%), which is still less than the high in 1994. The 'power' research increased early on, but begin decreasing later, until 1997. This implies that the concern about 'power' has been a hot topic in the recent past.[2] However, the slight waning of power studies suggests that new material needs to be made available to increase the understanding of the roots of 'power' in today's society – since violence remains and appears to becoming more violent and more random!

HOMICIDE VERSUS SUICIDE

Beyond the above actual domestic examples, there are national and international violence: prison brutality, seemingly random killings of thousands, neglect that leads to starvation of millions, discrimination, prejudice, religious conflicts, and more. Each morning we wake up to news of rapes that are more violent, murders and suicides for reasons we can not understand, killings by the thousands, and terrorist attacks. Homicide and suicide problems represent the ultimate in loss of control. The relationship of these problems can be observed in Figure 1, which shows the relative proportion of a psychiatric outpatient sample at intake that had mild to severe symptoms of anger.

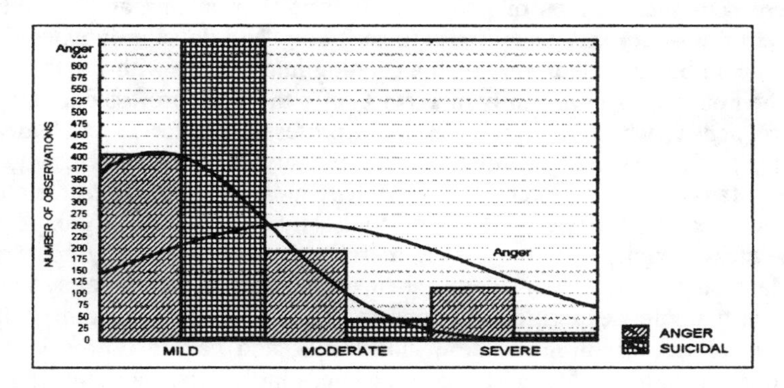

FIGURE 1. ANGER AND SUICIDAL CURVES FOR OUTPATIENTS.

Most often, suicide and homicide are two sides of the same coin. Suicide is the loss of control and powerlessness[3] and is frequently the result of the individual committing homicidal crimes, such as 21-year-old Benjamin Nathaniel Smith's drive-by killings in Illinois in July 1999, which ended in suicide. Figure 1 shows that as anger drops in numbers of individuals, suicidal tendencies also drop – more drastically, suggesting that anger and violence begin to replace suicidal thoughts and action as anger and violence increase in intensity. As anger gets more severe, suicidal tendencies lessen. Anger replaces suicide in the majority of violent individuals in the initial stage of acting on the aggression. When the outlet of anger is curtailed, suicide is the only violent act available to disperse the rampaging anger.

Society appears to do more to alleviate depression and suicide than anger. For example, we frequently see television ads about how to get psychological help for depression as well as ads for taking Prozac or some other anti-depressant drug. Such help is readily available in any community by mental health professionals. In contrast, it is difficult to find effective help for dealing with anger and violence. Typically, we deal with violence after the fact, and then we are forced to use "lock up" procedures through necessity, rather than offering professional help. The Pearson r correlation between depression and anger is .42, which is significantly high and suggests that as depression increases so does the potential for anger or vice versa. Many individuals committing violent acts also experience depression at the same time.

Beatings, brutality, neglect, and total disregard for the hurt and pain suffered by so many appear to be on the rise worldwide. One would have to surmise that there is a basic human desire to have power and control over others to such an extreme that many would like to render others helpless or dead for the sake of personal power. These dynamics represent the millions of people with control problems at all levels. Very few angry individuals tend to seek help, and do so only when the problem becomes extreme, such as getting into trouble with the law, or when others, such as family members, refer them for professional help. Frequently, when they are referred to professionals for psychological help by the court, they exhibit very little, if any, motivation for change.

Many political systems allow violent individuals to seize dictator positions. Such power directly or indirectly controls large groups of helpless people who they treat mercilessly and frequently murder. Many such individuals, whether their power rests in a national system[4] or in a single weapon, do not concern themselves about needing help. Control is everything to these individuals, and having power is the ultimate control. We read the consequences in the newspaper or hear it on the daily news, whether it is a single barbaric killing or an entire village massacred by a terrorist bomb.

Do We Understand Control Problems?

American and global emphasis in curtailing violence is after the fact. We wait until it happens and then we attempt to do something. Our efforts to do something are generally to strike back, put up barriers, lock up, and fence ourselves in with greater and greater security systems. What happened to understanding violence and engaging in early prevention? Would it not be better to look at the source of the problem and learn how to reduce the potential for violence wherever we can? As we have so frequently heard, we can not totally hide or protect ourselves from one who wants to do us harm. Ask a stalker victim, a rape victim, or a terrorist victim. Before long, we will all lose the feeling of 'safeness' and surround ourselves with barriers. As Hamlet so eloquently stated, we "lose the name of action" to reach out for any kind of normal life. Even the suit of armor did not help the knights for very long, nor was it without its unenviable attributes.

How does all this happen? Regardless of whether it is an individual, family, or a nation, it happens daily. At this writing, the news has just reported another Postal Worker shot and killed a co-worker on the job. Factors effecting money, position, and/or desperation relate to control and power. Two New York Times' bestsellers by David Baldacci are "Absolute Power" and "Total Control." Are we obsessed with power and control?

Most people want to have better self-control or self-discipline when dealing with such things as their temper, spouse, weather, appetite, kids, noise, road rage, airplane rage,[5] budget, boss, pain, congress, other people's values, country or world problems. While at the same time, individuals have a need to control groups of people, businesses, large corporations, and even nations. Frequently, the acquiring of rare paintings, antiques, or collecting the last Barbie doll or beanie baby is the manifestation of attempts at control. With control over others, there is status, respect, a guaranteed role, and security in the short term. Frequently, these acquisitions combine with the power of wealth or the illusion of wealth as well as cover over our profound personal insecurities.

Obviously, there are positive reinforcers for having control over others, even when carried too far. Many people, in all positions, do not understand their anger or temper and are not aware that they have such a problem or the effect it has on others. Some people say the political climate or system causes more power and an ideology develops to justify it. Some will attribute it to neighbors, their kids, the weather, religion, or anything around them. Others do not bother to attach it to anything. They are angry for reasons they do not understand and see this behavior as just the way they are or the way they were born and reared and do not want to acknowledge it.

Mental health workers frequently treat clients that have serious anger problems. Some patients have such serious anger problems that it causes them to pass out, incur migraines, or to lose their temper and kill someone. Some cause serious damage to property, others, or themselves. In one case, an individual stomped an electric fan to "death" because it would not work right. He broke eight bones in his foot! Some anger causes murder, and the individual still denies that they have a temper. The problem is not to simply treat control problems, but to understand why and how control exists in the first place. We must understand the complexity of control and the many forms it takes. We must learn to work for a balance of the components of control that allow us to gain power and control in our lives without building the negative drive of having or trying to have too much control. Everyone has control problems; it is just different for each person. The problem is finding out the pattern of control components for each person.

WHAT ARE THE CAUSES OF CONTROL PROBLEMS?

To get a handle on control problems, we need to understand the causes of control problems. Then, we need to understand what the loss of control means. Lastly, we need to learn some techniques to help develop more self-control or control over our environment. This book is about gaining control in a responsible way over almost all aspects of one's life *without over controlling* others. We examine the individual's responsibility in control problems, rather than the weapons used for controlling others. *If the need to control others is not there, neither are the weapons!*

We will look at the methods used by some to control others. We have examined individuals that attempted to maintain control by beating a helpless individual to death with tree limbs. Another individual killed their victim with a hammer. Another stabbed a helpless woman 27 times with a knife chasing her down the neighborhood street. A serial killer disembowels several helpless co-eds with a knife. Another shot an unarmed, unsuspecting man with a shotgun. Another let an infant starve to death. Another beat a relative to death with his fists. The common thread is not the method used to express the hostility, but the anger in the personality that was there and the loss of intense control. Anger may be released in a variety of ways, but can be understood with common denominators. Such concerns also include Stalin's Cold War, WWII holocaust, Jones Town, Charles Manson, Ted Bundy, Jeffrey Dohmer, Gary Gilmore, Waco, Pol Pot, and many other massive killings.

For example, Ted Bundy's serial killing continued in Seattle while he attended Law School in 1974 after moving away from his girlfriend and her daughter. The killings later spread across the country and ended in Miami in 1979 where he killed four sorority girls in a single rage after he had escaped from jail following a two-year incarceration. Prison time rarely teaches inmates anything about the ability to balance control problems appropriately. Bundy only learned from the deprivation of personal control how to exercise control over others when he escaped.

Ted had majored in psychology and lived with a girlfriend and her daughter in Washington. He was captured, but escaped from jail twice. Ted played verbal games with everyone and even acted in his own defense at his trial. He needed to control others, which he did verbally, using charm, and then he would beat his victims to death. The killings appeared to be some kind of obsessive-compulsive addictive outlet.

Following the killing, Ted would call his girlfriend. It was predicted that Ted would kill several girls after his second escape, because he lacked this violent outlet for two years. His victims were always attractive co-eds with long dark hair parted in the middle. He claims the number of his victims reached into three digits, but this has never been confirmed. Such claims add to the perpetrator's sense of control. Moreover, it was never confirmed that his victims were raped. We will learn more about the dynamics of such personalities after we learn about control.

Another massive killer is a man convicted of two murders in Oregon, and suspected in more than a dozen other killings. He was extradited to Kansas to face another murder charge. Robert Joseph Silveria, 39, known as the boxcar killer, was accused of bludgeoning Charles Russell Boyd to death in a collapsed tent at Kanopolis Lake's South Shore State Park in Ellsworth County, Kansas. According to court records, Boyd, who was in his 40s, met Silveria in El Paso, Texas, while Boyd was building a bunk house for a youth ranch, managed by 'Christ is the Answer' Mission. Silveria returned with him to the ranch and later traveled with him to Kansas.

When Boyd's body was discovered in July 1995, Silveria was no where to be found. Also missing were Boyd's identification, personal belongings, and vehicle. Silveria was arrested by a railroad police officer eight months later in Auburn, California. He had Boyd's credit cards with him at the time. Silveria was sentenced to life in prison for two murders in Oregon, and is a suspect in as many as 20 killing of boxcar riders throughout the country. Florida brought murder charges against him and authorities in Montana, Utah, Washington, and Arizona investigated a possible connection between Silveria and murders in their states. Police said he used birth certificates, Social Security cards, and the names of his victims' to obtain food stamps and other public assistance. Other killers such as 39-year-old Angel Maturino Resendez a/k/a Rafael Resendez-Ramirez was involved in railroad slayings as a rail-hopping drifter. He stole credentials for fake identities from individuals he killed until he turned himself in July 13, 1999, with the help of his family. He was responsible for at least nine killings

In addition, the investigation is still underway in the JonBenet Ramsay slaying and several other violent crimes at this writing. We have a situation in our own community were three co-eds have been missing for several years with no clues of what happened to them. The murderer has been tried and convicted. This circumstance exists in many cities and towns throughout America. Violence is committed by many different personalities of varying intelligence for many different reasons, and in countless ways.

Confinement Versus Prevention

Society appears to be directing its efforts more toward confinement of the perpetrator than prevention of the crime or even treatment of the perpetrator. Society wants revenge, which perpetuates the same violence with the high recidivism rates found for prisoners in the 1960s. We are quick to build more costly prisons, but we turn away from cheaper prevention. Perhaps it is true that some criminals are incurable, but the majority of prisoners are treatable. We can project, based on the increased number of persons in prison, that at some point in the future, we would all be in prison. Even knowing that projection, the pace of building new prisons continues. Who will be the guards? The psychology for the treatment process is available; however, we seem to be unable to link it to those in need. Prevention, at an early stage, is rarely considered. For example, consider the following idea.

Some practice of early prevention of control problems exists in some areas, but we are unaware of many effective programs. We recognize that functional family[6] knowledge has to start at the beginning of the child's life. In fact, it has to start when the mother is still pregnant. Mothers go through medical pre-natal training for the birth of the child. However, there is little, if any, psychological/family training at the pre- or post-natal stage of the child's development. Family training, linked to medical training for the mother, has great potential. Lecturettes,[7] tailored to include a developmental chronology of the child's early years, coping behaviors, and cast in a family system model, would demonstrate better adjustment effects for each family member for years to come.

We have to start somewhere. To begin educating the parent at any stage in their children's development can be beneficial. We have observed that, 'As the family goes, so goes the nation.' We are currently seeing the worst outcome of family dynamics and dysfunctional families ever known to the American culture. The above simple proposal will work. It fits everyone. People want to improve. It is not intrusive. The medical side of the process is already in place in many hospitals. Support groups would include County Nurses, Police Departments, Chambers of Commerce, School systems, all Social Agencies, all Providers, Businesses, Universities, Churches, and Health Insurance groups. They will all benefit from the positive outcomes.

INCREASED EMPHASIS ON SECURITY SYSTEMS

When we are not locking people up, we are getting more suspicious, paranoid, and paying larger sums of money to protect ourselves. In Wichita Kansas, a plastic box found near the entrance of the Sedgwick County Zoo was thought to be a bomb. After much time, anxiety, and expense it was discovered to be a first-aid kit!

Sheriff's Department Capt. Mitchell Paige said firefighters participating in the Children's Fair at the zoo found the box around one p.m. April 17, 1998. "They put it on a bench and contacted security," Paige said, according to the media. "It had a padlock on it, so they were not sure of what it was."

X-rays showed the box contained metal objects, wires, batteries and a bottle of liquid, and such items could indicate a bomb, Paige said. Consequently, authorities sealed off the area, more than three hundred yards. About 13,000 visitors were evacuated to the parking lot. The visitors stood around and watched for about two hours before allowed to go home. Most of the animals of the zoo were outside of the secured perimeter. Traffic near the zoo was re-routed.

The bomb squad used a special water gun to 'detonate' the suspected bomb. The water gun shot a concentrated, high-speed jet at the box, which caused the box to come apart, and they discovered that it was a box of first-aid materials. Some bandages, a bottle of antiseptic cream and a flashlight were reported to be among the contents.

How much in time, effort, and cost was involved for thousands of people in the several hours it took to find that someone accidentally left a first-aid box near the entrance of the zoo. We hear incidents of children being suspended from school when they take their medicine because of "no drug" policies. Are we going too far and how far it that? How do we know? Again, we are dealing with situations as either black or white with no one trained to distinguish the in-between levels. Where will it lead?

The nation's adult federal, state prisons, and jail inmates grew to more than 1.8 million men and women by the end of 1998, up almost 5 percent from 1997. Prison population growth comes from inmates serving longer terms for violent crimes and a steady stream of criminals entering prison doors, according to an August 1998 report from the Justice Department. There has been a 6.7 percent annual average increase in prison population during the 90's, according to the department's Bureau of Justice statistics. If this growth continues, the combined prison population will top two million by the year 2000 – although crime has been dropping since 1994. The increased time served, particularly for violent crimes, is a product of tougher parole boards, longer minimum sentences, and truth-in-sentencing laws that require more of each sentence to be served in prison rather than on parole. These tougher sentencing laws and parole rulings pushed the U.S. incarceration rate up from one out of every 217 residents in 1990 to one of every 149 in 1998, the bureau reported. The last prison decline was in 1972.

Our society clearly believes that 'lockup' is the only key to solving crime. Perhaps we believe 'lockup' is easier. Our question is. "How much hard and direct money are we spending on the prevention of crime and the rehabilitation of criminals?" Have we given up? In many states, there are no psychological/psychiatric services of qualified and licensed mental health professionals working in prison systems. This has not changed significantly in the last 75 years, although mental health practices have appeared on the scene and have shown great advances in all areas!

Chapter 2 details crime and population statistics, characteristics of crime, and many other aspects of crime to help us assess the size and dimensions of violence.

---

[1] American Psychological Society Observer, Report 5, October 1997.

[2] Berle, A.A. 1967. *Power*, New York: Harcourt, Brace & World, Inc. David C McClelland. 1975. *Power: The inner experience*, Irvington Publishers, Inc., New York.

[3] Tiffany, D.W. and Tiffany, P.G. 1973. Social unrest: Powerlessness and/or Self-Direction? *American Psychologist*, 28, 151-154.

[4] Buckley, W. 1968. *Modern systems research for the behavioral scientist: A sourcebook.* ed. Chicago: Aldine Publishing Co.

[5] Government statistics indicate that 25 percent of airplane rage involves alcohol; 16 percent, disputes over seating assignments; 10 percent, smokers who are prohibited from smoking; nine percent, carry-on luggage disputes; eight percent, problems with flight attendants; and five percent, food concerns.

[6] Tiffany, D.W., Cohen, J., Ogburn, K., and Robinson, A. eds. 1975. *Helping families to change.* New York: Aronson Press. (Translated into Dutch.)

[7] Brief lectures when mothers come in for medical examinations.

Chapter 2: Crime Statistics

A FBI crime report[8] in 1995 on domestic homicides found that husbands or boyfriends killed 26 percent of all female murder victims. Wives or girlfriends killed three percent of male murder victims.

Los Angeles and New York reported preliminary crime data for 1996. Los Angeles had 688 homicides through December 14, 1996, compared to 829 for the same period in 1995. City officials said a drop in domestic homicides was part of the decline. Some feel that the publicity of spousal abuse has helped to cut down on spousal homicides.

New York City, too, has had a huge overall drop in violent crime. After decades of increases, the number of murders in the city in 1996 dropped sharply to less than half the number in 1990. Most of the drop was due to declines in murders by strangers. In 1993, for instance, 37 percent of murders in New York City were committed by strangers and 63 percent by acquaintances. In 1995, 19 percent of the city murders were committed by strangers and 81 percent by acquaintances.

Some city officials analyzed preliminary data for 1996 and noted drops in local domestic homicides. Data reported to the FBI by local law enforcement officials' show that the nation's crime rate dropped by three percent in the first half of 1996, and the number of murders declined by seven percent. The largest drops in violent crime were in big cities. A few (Atlanta, Las Vegas, Miami, and Washington, DC) registered increases in homicides. Rapes reported throughout the nation dropped by one percent.

Violent crimes include rape, robbery, aggravated and simple assault, and homicide. "Serious crime reported to the police nationwide in 1997 declined for a sixth consecutive year, with reduction in every region led by a plunge of more than 10 percent in murder in larger cities and suburban counties," as reported by Michael J. Sniffen of the Associated Press. There were exceptions. In Wichita and Topeka,

Kansas, for example, the same statistics told a very different story. The number of aggravated assaults in both cities rose by more than 13 percent. Wichita reported 1,298 aggravated assaults in 1996 and 1,481 in 1997. Topeka reported 863 in 1996 and 979 in 1997.

Nationally, violent crimes of murder, rape, robbery, and aggravated assault dropped five percent. Far more numerous property crimes of burglary, auto theft, and larceny-theft, dipped four percent. The most dramatic declines were in murder, for which statistics are the most reliable and uniform. Homicide was down nine percent nationwide, but 14 percent in cities of 250,000 to 500,000; 11 percent in cities over one million and in suburban counties; and 10 percent in cities of 500,000 to one million people. However, we must recognize that although violence is down, the characteristics of violence are sometimes more hideous (e.g., decapitations) and it is breaking out in traditionally safe areas, such as work and school. In addition, the media disseminates more details in murder cases than in the past.

CHARACTERISTICS OF CRIME

Characteristics of crime as summarized in 1995 for violent crime and victim/offender relationship reveals the following. If we exclude those crimes in which the victim/offender relationship was unknown, 52 percent of persons victimized by nonfatal violence did not know their assailant. Strangers, compared to 3 out of 10 of all rapes/sexual assaults, committed seven out of ten robberies. Just over one-third of all rapes/sexual assaults were committed by nonrelatives well known to the victim.

For murder victims, 45 percent were related to or acquainted with their assailants: strangers murdered 15 percent of victims, while almost 40 percent of victims had an unknown relationship to their murderer. Intimate violence showed the following patterns.

In 1996, women experienced an estimated 840,000 rape, sexual assault, robbery, aggravated assault and simple assault victimization at the hands of an intimate, down from 1.1 million in 1993. Intimate violence against men did not vary significantly from 1992 to 1996.

On average, from 1976-1996, the number of murders by intimates decreased by 5 percent per year for male victims and one percent per year for female victims.

The sharpest decrease in rates of intimate murder has been for black male victims.

Intimate violence is primarily a crime against women – in 1996, females were the victims of three of every four victims of intimate murder and about 85 percent of the victims of nonlethal intimate violence.

Women age 16-24 experience the highest per capita rates of intimate violence.

Concerning the time of occurrence of the crime, it was found that while overall violent crimes were more likely to occur during the day than at night, some crimes exhibited different patterns. For example, 54 percent of incidents of violent crime occurred between 6 a.m. and 6 p.m. Approximately two thirds of rapes/sexual assaults occurred at night – 6 p.m. to 6 a.m.

About 25 percent of incidents of violent crimes in 1995 occurred at or near the victim's home. Among common locales for violent crimes were streets other than those near the victim's home (19 percent), at school (14 percent), or at a commercial establishment (12 percent). In addition, 23 percent of victims of violent crime reported being involved in some from of leisure activity away from home at the time of their victimization. Twenty-one percent said they were at home, and another 21 percent mentioned they were at work or traveling to or from work when the crime occurred. One in four violent crimes occurred in or near the victim's home. Including these, almost half occurred within a mile from home and 73 percent within five miles. Only 4 percent of victims of violent crime reported that the crime took place more than 50 miles from their home.

The Bureau of Justice Statistics provides a summary of victim characteristics for 1996. (1) They found that one in 11 were age 12 to 15, compared to one in 100, age 65 or more. (2) One in 19 were blacks, compared to one in 25 were white and (3) one in 20 males, compared to one in 29 were females.

WEAPON USE

In one-quarter of the incidents of violent crime, offenders used or threatened to use a weapon. National Crimes Victimization Survey defines assaults involving weapons as aggravated: thus, almost all aggravated assaults (95 percent) involved a weapon. Assaults without weapons are classified as aggravated if the victim suffers a serious injury. Offenders had or used a weapon in slightly more than half of all robberies, compared with 5 percent of all rapes/sexual assaults.

ROLE OF ALCOHOL IN CRIME VICTIMIZATION

About three million violent crimes occur each year in which victims perceive the offender to have been drinking at the time of the offense. Among those victims who provided information about the offender's use of alcohol, about 35 percent of the victimization cases involved an offender who had been drinking. Two-thirds of victims who suffered violence by an intimate (a current or former spouse, boyfriend, or girlfriend) reported that alcohol had been a factor.

Among spouse victims, three out of four incidents were reported to have involved an offender who had been drinking. By contrast, an estimated 31 percent of stranger victimization, where the victim could determine the absence or presence of alcohol was perceived to be alcohol-related. For about one in five violent victimization cases involving perceived alcohol use by the offender, victims also reported they believed the offender to have been using drugs as well.

DOMESTIC VIOLENCE

Linda David, 50, had not been seen for years and was rescued from having been crammed into the bow of her husband's "putrid, scum-stained sailboat" in 1997 by police in Everett, about 25 miles north of Seattle, Washington. Mrs. David was kept prisoner and forced to lie among dog feces from six German shepherds, that also lived on the 30-foot boat. Mrs. Linda's nose was distorted and bulbous, her ears were cauliflowered, her face was covered with knots and bruises. Doctors indicated her limbs were deformed by years of untreated fractures. It took two and one-half years, until May of 1999, before her husband, Victor David, 59, was charged with assault, who could get up to 10 years in prison for the abuse of his wife! Even worst, state records had indicated that Mrs. David was suspected of being abused as early as 1983 and that a doctor had urged welfare workers to look in on the matter. Mrs. David's husband was collecting $450 a month in state money saying she suffered from multiple sclerosis and was injured from falling out of a truck. Her family believes Mr. David abused her before they were married in 1980. A welfare agent who had not heard from her for at least three years discovered Mrs. David. He went to the boat to check on her and then called police because the boat smelled so bad. The police officers had to wear masks. Mrs. David now lives in a nursing home where she bears the evidence of "very, very hard" beatings by her husband.

How frightened can a person feel? Some individuals never get the feeling of "safeness" back in their life. Mrs. David said there was "No way I could get off to get help...That was home. I never had anywhere else." No one should ever have to experience that much fear for a protracted period. However, this is not an isolated case. There are almost six times as many women victimized by intimates (18%), as those victimized by strangers (3%), who did not report their violent victimization to police because they feared reprisal from the offender. This is what happened to Mrs. David. In 1994, women experienced 572,032 violent victimization at the hands of an intimate, compared to

48,983 incidents committed against men, according to Dr. R. Bachman[9]. These U.S. statistics appeared in a 1994 report, "Violence Against Women: A National Crime Victimization Survey Report." According to Dr. Bachman, someone known to the women committed over two-thirds of violent victimization against them: 31% of female victims reported that the offender was a stranger. Approximately 28% were intimates such as husbands or boyfriends, 35% were acquaintances, and the remaining 5% were other relatives. In contrast, victimization by intimates and other relatives accounted for only 5% of all violent victimization against men. Men were significantly more likely to have been victimized by acquaintances (50%) or strangers (44%) than by intimates or other relatives.

Battered women seek medical attention for injuries sustained as a consequence of domestic violence significantly more often after separation than during cohabitation; about 75% of the visits to emergency rooms by battered women occur after separation.

Many people are in relationships that make them feel concerned or uncomfortable because it is not always obvious when a relationship is becoming abusive. Domestic violence is not something that happens suddenly. Usually a pattern evolves over time. It often begins with some form of controlling behavior, which leads to greater and greater control and then violence. The National Domestic Violence Hotline is 1-800-799-SAFE (or 7233). The TDD for the Hearing-Impaired is 1-800-787-3224. Women Against Abuse made a list of warning signs to help you understand whether or not you are in an abusive relationship. If the person you love does any of the following to you, call the domestic abuse hotline.

⇒ **Constantly keeps track of your time,**

⇒ **Acts jealous and possessive,**

⇒ **Accuses you of being unfaithful or flirting,**

⇒ **Discourages your relationships with friends and family,**

⇒ **Prevents you from working or attending school,**

⇒ **Constantly criticizes you,**

⇒ **Controls all finances and demands accountability of your expenses,**

⇒ **Humiliates you in front of others,**

⇒ **Destroys personal property or sentimental items,**

⇒ **Threatens to hurt you or your children with or without a weapon,**

⇒ **Pushes, hits, slaps, punches, kicks, or bites you or your children, or**

⇒ **Forces you to have sex against your will.**

PROPERTY CRIMES

Of the almost 4.8 million house burglaries in 1995, 4.1 million, or 84 percent, were completed burglaries. In the remaining 0.8 million (16 percent), the offender attempted forcible entry. In a third of the completed burglaries, the burglar forced entry into the home; in two-thirds, the burglar gained entry through an unlocked door or open window. Of the 22 million completed thefts of property, there were 8.2 million (39 percent) property thefts of less than $50, 7.6 million (36 percent) between $50 and $249, 4.1 million (20 percent) of $250 or more, and for 1.2 million (5 percent) the property value was unknown.

CRIMES BY CHILDREN

School-associated violent deaths are involving multiple victims, according to an article in the August 1998 American Psychological Association Monitor. If we examine the bizarre school murders, we find the following number of deaths, which range from zero to fifteen from 1993 to the winter of 1999. The linear regression suggests that the problem is increasing at a rapid pace. It is scary for one to contemplate where this could lead, particularly with individuals being apprehended for threatening to blow up schools as well as assassinate many students and teachers.

Figure 2 shows that recent years have seen a rash of school shootings that has accounted for killings (including teachers) in the double digits and about an equal number wounded. The year 1999 only extends to the end of April. The trend seems to be increasing. Children from ages 11 to 17 carried out these killings.

One of the schoolyard killings was at Jonesboro, Arkansas by an 11 and a 13-year-old boy. It was 12:35 p.m. when the 11-year-old pulled a fire alarm inside Westside Elementary School and then he joined the 13-year-old in a nearby wooden area. Students and teachers filed out of the school onto the school ground and the doors locked behind them. At that point, the two boys opened fire from the woods about 100 yards away. The boys, armed with three rifles and seven handguns, got off 22 shots in about four minutes. They killed four girls and one teacher and wounded nine students and one teacher. The police captured the two boys within 15 minutes of the shooting.

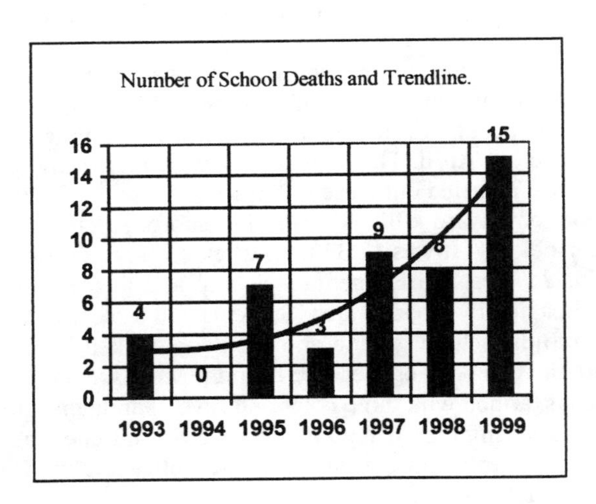

FIGURE 2. NUMBER OF SCHOOL DEATHS FROM 1993 TO 1999

As of this writing, the most recent school shooting took place at Columbine High School in Littleton, Colorado on April 20, 1999 about 11:30 AM when two heavily armed students dressed in black stormed the school. The bloody rampage left 12 students (eight boys and four girls) and one teacher dead and 23 others were wounded. Then the two shooters shot themselves in the head. They left behind scenes of incredible carnage on the stairwells, cafeteria, and the library. The killing was savage with casual cruelty. A 15-year-old reported that one of the schoolgirls was hiding under a desk and he said "Peek-a-boo" to her and promptly shot her in the neck. One shooter called out, "All the jocks stand up – I'm going to kill every single one of you." It was reported that the shooters, "were laughing, hooting, and hollering." Hundreds of students scrambled from the school while others barricaded themselves in classrooms and restrooms searching for safe hiding from rapid gunfire and many explosives the shooters used. SWAT teams used armored cars to gain entrance to the school and then crept through the high school searching for the gunmen and wounded students while helping other students escape.

The two shooters responsible for the deadliest school shooting in American history were Erik Harris, age 18, and Dylan Klebold, age 17, who are alleged to have broken at least 18 current gun laws. They were members of the "trench coat Mafia" at Columbine. There is some suspicion that the shooters may have had some help in placing some of the 30 bombs found after the massacre.

A new Washington Post-ABC news poll of teen-agers and parents was reported in April 22-25, 1999. They found that about a third of teen-agers questioned had heard a student threaten to kill someone. A fifth of the teen-agers knew someone who had brought a gun to school. Out of the 500 public and private high school students and 522 parents who were interviewed, more than eight out of 10 said they feel relatively safe from school violence.

In response to the explosive nature of recent school shootings, questions are raised about "What is the minimum age a child can be tried as an adult?" Twenty-seven states have no minimum age. The other states use 15 (Louisiana) to seven (New York) as the minimum age. Many articles appeared in magazines and newspapers across the country to dissect the cause and understand such personalities. The great majority of pre-adolescent, adolescent, and teenage children have enough self-control to avoid committing such atrocious acts. The question must be raised about the responsibility of the parents of those who commit such heinous crimes. Children do not grow up in a vacuum – or do they in some cases?

In some cases, the violent child says others bullied him and he was seeking revenge. In other cases, it is simple entitlement of doing whatever we please if things do not go our way, or it was parental neglect and the influence of violent computer games or movies. Now there is talk about criminal prosecution against the parents for gross neglect of parental duty, which absolves the child, at any age, of responsibility. How responsible is a child – at any age?

After a high school shooting spree in Springfield, Oregon, May 21, 1998 by 15 year-old, Kipland P. Kinkel, it was discovered he had already killed both parents at home. Both parents were teachers. Both parents were killed the day before the shooting spree took place. Two students died and 22 students were wounded or hurt. Two of the students were in critical condition. It is not now possible to hold Kip's parents accountable, but it was found that he had been expelled from school the day before because of the possession of a firearm. It has been reported that 70 percent of school shootings have been by children who have been known to previously bring guns to school.

Kip was known to have a history of violence and was voted as the student 'most likely to start WWIII.' Other kids and the teachers knew that Kip had serious problems. In fact, he was on Prozac and was referred to 'anger management' counseling. The number of sessions Kip attended is unknown. Nor do we know what the qualifications were of the person conducting such counseling. Such counseling conducted by qualified professionals can be very effective. A wounded student, Jake Ryker, who was shot in the chest and left hand, finally subdued Kip, and when wrestled to the floor, Kip cried, "Go ahead and kill me."

Our thesis throughout this book is that violence is frequently situation-specific. Although the individual completes a few sessions of counseling for anger management, the situation driving the problem may still be present, such as the closed system of the school, and not dealt with in the counseling.

Who should take the responsibility of reporting such youth problems to authorities? It should be completed before kids like Kip kill four people, cause injuries to 22 others, and then when in custody take a stab at a police officer with a hunting knife he had taped to his leg. Teachers, school administrators, and parents should report these incidents to any authorities involved. What responsibility should his peers take? Many of them knew about Kip's sophisticated bomb making knowledge, his more-than-average interest in guns, and his history of animal torturing, and other delinquent acts such as dropping rocks on cars from an overpass.

Peer group members run into the problem of being identified as 'snitches.' On May 19, 1998 near Clearfield, Pennsylvania, a 15-year-old girl's body was found by hikers in a clearing called Gallows Harbor – named after a hanging there in the 19th century – about five miles from Clearfield. Kimberly Jo Dotts was strung up in a tree. A 'friend' clubbed her to death with a rock, for backing out of a plan and threatening to reveal the plan of the group of teens to run away to Florida. At one point, the teenagers pulled Kimberly Jo around the wooded clearing by her neck. The third time the rope was put around her neck, Kimberly Jo was hung from a tree for several minutes until she lost consciousness, then taken down. When she continued to move someone struck her with a four-inch rock.

A week before Kimberly Jo was found, her mother had placed a missing-person's ad in a newspaper describing her daughter as five feet one inch tall and 165 pounds. Kimberly Jo was called a 'snitch.' Several of the teens involved were placed in custody and charged with homicide.

Is Kimberly Jo's fate what happens to peers that try to do the right thing? Have our values become that distorted or are they totally absent? Who has the courage to be responsible? Self-Directed individuals are capable of escaping from violence, but are they capable of preventing it? Self-Directed characteristics are discussed more fully later.

Astor and Behre published a paper in 1997[10] that discussed violent and nonviolent children's and parents' reasoning about family and peer violence. The authors used 17 violent boys (age 10 years, seven months to 13 years, 10 months) with emotional and behavioral disorders and their aggressive parents (18 subjects). All the children had committed lethal or potentially lethal violent acts before age 10. The results of the study revealed that violent children and their parents were more likely to react to violent scenarios referring to rules prohibiting provocation (External Control, stopping conflict in the first place), than to rules prohibiting physical retribution (leaning Self-Control after being assaulted). The significance of these findings will become more obvious from Chapter 4 when we separate the sources of control. Astor and Behre's study point up the bias in differences in perceiving cause when violence is involved. We perceive according to our training and experience.

What responsibility should be taken with adolescent and teen violence? Whatever the cause, it comes down to responsible self-disciplined behavior that can be learned, but for many people, professional intervention becomes a necessity that should only be undertaken with **qualified** professionals! Kip was trained in Karate and claimed he had excellent self-control! Obviously, he was not very responsible or value anchored to appropriate Self-Direction!

Our greatest hope is that some day the value of psychotherapy, in the hands of a qualified professional, will be recognized as a viable recourse for treating violence. Such treatment is currently available. All too often, we look at mental health treatment as something anyone can administer, or, we believe such professionals cannot handle problems of violence! That is a gross error and the public needs to be better educated to the effectiveness of psychological treatment. There are limited applications for mental health professionals who do not have a doctorate in the mental health field, just like there are limited applications in the medical field if the individual did not complete a medical degree. Treating violence is not one of the limited applications, and even qualified professionals need special training in treating individuals with problems of violence.

Instead of such referrals, local schools have sounded alarms all across the country. Headlines in the Lawrence Journal-World, section B, on May 29, 1998 proclaimed, "Wave of violence hits area schools." A 13-year-old seventh-grader had been taken from an area school in handcuffs after several fellow students said he repeatedly threatened to kill them. He was initially put in a Detention Center in Leavenworth. No gun or other weapons were found in his home, locker, or school bags and no one knows where the rumor came from that he had a gun or other weapon. The school Superintendent, Richard Erickson, said he hopes the boy's arrest will deter other students who might contemplate threats against others. According to Erickson, "He had threatened six or seven other students, indicated verbally to the students he would kill them." He added, "we're taking a very strong stand on threats of violence." After an emergency meeting by the local school board members, they decided to close schools three days early after rumors of the threats. Erickson stated, "We'll take a strong stand now and in the future. It's important to send a strong message to students." Such actions has been reported by many schools.

The recent barrage of school assaults against teachers and students has put everyone on edge and caused such jitters that 'everyone wants to close the shop and run.' Our detection methods of who is likely to cause such problems and who is just mouthing off out of frustration are rarely applied. Consequently, we chose the simplest route and just shut down. The pendulum always seems to swing from knowing nothing and doing nothing to over reacting about almost anything. Eventually it will reach the middle point of prevention by ferreting out the child with a problem and treating such individuals on a case by case basis, whether it includes lockup or treatment or both. In addition, as will be noted below, out tendency is to use environmental pressures to subdue anger rather than teach self-control so that it is never discharged in the first place – whether as a threat or actual violence. The result of the incident cited earlier will be school crimes falling on the shoulders of this and other 13-year-olds, who did not even have assess to a weapon. What will be the damage to them for the sake of making a point to the other children? How does it solve the problem? It simply increased the environmental stress on everyone. This additional form of controlling all the children is not what is needed. This is a throwback to the old philosophy that "children should be seen and not heard." We will see later why this form of control only increases the anger.

One reader of the newspaper responded to the headlines "Wave of violence hits area schools," with an editorial stating that there was "no 'wave' and that, in fact, there wasn't even any violence." He cited the U.S. Office of Technology Assessment as reporting that children were in far greater danger[11] off school grounds than in schools. Obviously, a lot of national policy is driven by fears rather than actual data, which in no way undermine the importance of our concern over the rash of school shootings.

W. Rodney Hammond, Ph.D. is a psychologist who heads violence-prevention efforts for the Center for Disease Control and Prevention in Atlanta. He states that "Many scientists believe that if we try, based on our present knowledge, to invent a screening tool to identify who's at risk for engaging in a homicidal act, we would probably identify a lot of kids who engage in antisocial behavior but who may not kill." Dr. Hammond fails to recognize that very few new concepts in testing have been developed over the last 40 years in psychometrics. These circumstances would seem to set the stage for looking at new screening techniques. One concept, well known in psychology, is the important part that situations play in personality evaluation and, in particular, where violence is concerned. Yet, the only standardized and computerized test, to our knowledge, that is anchored to situations and control problems and can be customized to fit any context is the Tiffany Control Scales. This test is discussed in more detailed in later chapters and in many of the Endnote references.

FEMALES AS INDEPENDENT CRIMINALS

According to Knight Ridder Newspapers, more girls are becoming independent criminals. Between 1992 and 1996, the violent crime arrest rate for girls increased by 25 percent while the rate for boys remained steady, based on data from the National Center for Juvenile Justice. However, between 1983 and 1992, the arrest rate for violent crimes among girls under 18 increased by 85 percent while for boys, it went up by 50 percent. Apparently, equal rights are clearly an equal opportunity for criminal behavior!

In the past, girls would usually commit crimes with boys or men. Now, they are calling their own shots. "Clearly, today we are seeing a trend of women initiating the criminality: women as masterminds, women as predators," said Michael Rustigan, professor of criminology at San Francisco State University.

HATE CRIMES

The U.S. Department of Justice, Criminal Justice Information Services Division, reports the preliminary figures for hate crimes. The data show 7,947 hate crime incidents were reported to the FBI during 1995. Incidents reported were by more than 9,500 law enforcement agencies in 45 states and the District of Columbia. Participating agencies covered 75 percent of the U.S. The top four states reporting hate crimes were California (1,751), New York (845), New Jersey (768), and Michigan (405). The five top Bias Motivation by Incident reports were for Race (4,831 reports; 6,438 victims), Anti-Black (2,988 reports; 3,945 victims), Religion (1,277 reports; 1,617 victims), Anti-White (1,226 reports; 1,554 victims), and Anti-Jewish (1,058 reports; 1,236 victims). One would have to surmise that the more different we look the less tolerance there is for differences! Could it mean we really need a society of clones? Remember Dr. Suess's allegory about the Star-Bellied Sneeches, where a machine was invented to make everyone look alike. The problem was that some Sneeches wanted to look different and they had to invent another machine to remove what the first machine added. So it goes, right into the twenty-first century! How do we erase stereotypes?

The statistics show that 61 percent of the hate incidents were motivated by racial bias; 16 percent by religious bias; 13 percent by sexual-orientation bias; and 10 percent by ethnicity/national origin bias. The 7,947 incidents involved 9,895 separate offenses, 10,469 victims, and 8,433 known offenders. Crimes against persons accounted for 72 percent of hate crime offenses reported. Intimidation was the single most frequently reported hate crime offense, accounting for 41 percent of the total. Damage/destruction/vandalism of property constituted 23 percent; simple assault, 18 percent; and aggravated assault, 13 percent. Twenty persons were murdered in personal hate-motivated incidents. An example is 16-year-old Adrianne Jones, who was murdered by Diane Zamora and David Graham, two bright U.S. military academy students, on the belief that David had sex with Adrianne when they were still in high school.

As in previous years, hate crimes in 1995 were most frequently directed at individuals. Individuals comprised 83 percent of all reported bias crime victims for the year, which was equal to 7,144 victims. Businesses, religious organizations, and varied other targets comprised the remaining 17 percent. There is no breakout of stalking crimes, which are more often than not, hate crimes. However, Fremouw, Westrup, and Pennypacker (1997)[12] conducted a study of "Stalking on Campus." The authors administered 299 questionnaires to college undergraduates and found that 30 percent of the female students and 17 percent of male students reported having been stalked. Eighty percent reported that they knew their stalker. Only one percent of the subjects admitted having stalked someone. The most common response by females was to ignore the stalker, while the males confronted the stalker.

Law enforcement agencies reported the number of known offenders for 62 percent of crimes involving hate coming to their attention in 1995. Among the 8,433 known offenders reported to be associated with hate crime incidents, 59 percent were white, and 27 percent were black. The remaining offenders were of other multi-racial groups.

An example of a hideous hate crime was committed near Jasper, Texas on June 9, 1998, as reported by the Associated Press. Three white men with suspected ties to the Ku Klux Klan chained a black hitchhiker, James Byrd, Jr., age 49, to the back bumper of a pickup truck and dragged him to his death. Byrd's head, neck, and right arm were found about a mile from his mangled torso. Byrd had been dragged about two miles on a narrow, winding asphalt road. Byrd had been walking home from a niece's bridal shower on a Saturday night and apparently accepted a ride from the three men. When he was found, he was so badly disfigured that investigators had to use fingerprints to identify him. There were 75 red spray-painted circles along the road to mark where police had found either Byrd's belongings – his keys and dentures – or body parts. The chain believed to be used to drag him was found behind a house. Two of the perpetrators were covered with tattoos indicating white supremacist beliefs, and all three had spend time in prison. They apparently had ties to the Ku Klux Klan and the Aryan Nation, according to Sheriff Billy Rowles.

The above U.S. statistics do not reflect the international scene of violence regarding hate crimes. For instance, the Associated Press reported on May 7, 1998 that the extreme-right has been gaining ground across Europe, playing on anti-foreigner sentiments. They reported that the trend is especially disturbing in Germany with neo-Nazism. Following the far right's best ever showing in a state election in postwar Germany, federal officials confirmed May 6 1998 that right wing violence is on the rise – especially in the former communist east. The office for the Protection of the Constitution, which monitors extremist groups, recorded 790 right-wing attacks last year – 27 percent more than in 1996 and the first increase in four years. Most of the attacks involved young men beating up foreigners, whom the skinheads and new-Nazis accuse of stealing jobs from Germans or of milking the welfare state. Half the attacks occurred in depressed eastern Germany, although the region accounts for less than a fifth of Germany's 82 million people and roughly 5 percent of its 7.4 million foreigners. Overall, some 11,700 right wing offenses were recorded in 1997, believed to be a postwar record. Nearly 90 percent involved neo-Nazi propaganda that is banned in Germany, ranging from painted swastikas on walls to distributing CDs by skinhead bands. A professional friend of ours recently shared with us that he avoids using English in East Berlin for fear of his life.

A more recent hate crime, designed "To be a wake-up call to America to kill Jews," according to the white supremacist Buford O. Furrow, age 37. He walked into a FBI office August 11, 1999 and confessed to recent shootings. He wounded five individuals (five-year-old boy, two six-year-old boys, a 16-year-old girl, and a 68-year-old adult, the Center receptionist) at the North Valley Jewish Community Center in Los Angeles. He also confessed to shooting a Filipino-American postal worker the same day. Reports note that Furrow had frequented the Aryan Nation compound in Idaho where he may have been a security guard. He revealed to the FBI that he had tried to commit himself to a psychiatric hospital the year before the shootings.

When supremacists point to the Bible to justify hate, are they also experiencing a mental illness of some kind?

It appears that some groups, regardless of national origin, race, or whatever, detest differences in others. Should we prejudge others by our makeup and if found to differ, should they be excluded and ultimately assaulted? The answer is obvious; however, one example is a gang-related murder that took place in Buffalo, Missouri. Five young people claiming to be members of a violent street gang with roots in Los Angeles beat Michael Sutton, age 20, so viciously he suffered a brain hemorrhage. Then they slit his throat and left him bleeding to death under a bridge outside of town. All this happened because Michael wanted to quit the Five Deuce Hoover Crips street gang. Apparently, he was not allowed to be different. He was a member and had to stay a member. Is this cause for malicious violence? You would have to be seriously mentally ill if you thought it was. Gangs are closed systems and are only comfortable if they "own" their members.

Many theorists and researchers have sought an explanation of this kind of prejudice and violence without fully understanding the perceptional distortion that takes place. This left them with empty explanations of why violence continues to be such a dominant human trait. We would like to examine addition real events throughout this book and attempt an explanation of prejudice and bias that reaches violent proportions.

MENTAL ILLNESS AND VIOLENCE

John Hinkley wounded President Ronald Reagan and James Brady. Hinkley was captured and found mentally ill. What is the role of mental illness in violence? The day following July 24, 1998, we read the headlines, "Two Slain at Capitol." A lone gunman from Montana broke through heavy security at the tourist-packed Capital building in Washington, DC. He unleashed a torrent of gunshots, exchanging fire with police and killing two Capital police officers (Jacob Chestnut and John Gibson) before he was shot. A female tourist was seriously wounded in the exchange of gunfire. The gunman, Russell Eugene Weston, Jr. was described as a delusional paranoid schizophrenic drifter. He was considered a threat to the president and feared his neighbor's satellite dish. His father reportedly told him to get out of the house for killing more than a dozen cats at his father's home the day before he killed the two police officers. His bizarre behavior drew immediate comparisons to another high-profile Montana resident, known for his violent behavior, the Unabomber, Theodore Kaczynski.

The 41-year-old Weston apparently drifted between his home in Valmeyer, Illinois and Montana. In Montana, he lived in a 10 by 12-

foot plywood shack in the woods about 60 miles north of Helena, about 40 miles from where Kaczynski lived. The Secret Service interviewed Weston in April 1996, subsequently, a psychological assessment was ordered. He was committed for two months to a mental hospital in Montana. It was determined that he was not imminently dangerous. Weston was prescribed medication after his release, but it was said he did not renew the two-week prescription.

Assessing danger to self or others is sometimes impossible. A psychotic is not psychotic all the time. Rarely can we assess the level of severity of the delusions and the precipitating circumstances or thoughts, or when he or she might be experiencing delusions that would lead to violence. In addition, situational factors frequently add to the stress-inducing factors, which must also be part of the assessment. For example, after Weston killed a dozen cats or more in his hometown of Valmeyer with a shotgun, his father kicked him out of the house. Such additional stress will add to Weston's delusional system and, consequently, to the level of potential violence. Later, it was also learned that he had stolen his father's 38-caliber Smith & Wesson revolver – possibly the handgun used in the Capital shooting. This information would generally be enough for a qualified mental health worker to recommend extreme caution to anyone involved with Weston.

According to the U.S. Justice Department's report from the Bureau of Justice Statistics in July 1999 by Michael J. Sniffen, Associated Press, the nation's prisons and jails held an estimated 283,800 mentally ill inmates in 1998. They also estimated that an additional 547,800 mentally ill offenders have been released on probation into communities. These estimates did not include anyone committed to a hospital after a verdict of not guilty by reason of insanity or anyone civilly committed to a mental hospital. The study concluded that the mentally ill were more likely than other offenders to have committed violent offenses. For example, in state prisons, 53 percent of mentally ill inmates, compared with 46 percent of the other inmates, were locked up for violent crimes. Among federal inmates, 33 percent of the mentally ill, but only 13 percent of other inmates had violent offenses. Among local jail inmates, 30 percent of the mentally ill, but only 26 percent of the other inmates, had committed violent crimes. Lastly, among probationers, 28 percent of the mentally ill, but only 18 percent of the other inmates reported their current offense was violent. It was found that more than twice the percentage of mentally ill inmates reported prior physical or sexual abuse than did other inmates.

Paula Ditton, author of the study and bureau statistician stated that "This does not mean that mentally ill offenders are more violent than other offenders." There could be other causes for these self-reported figures. For example, police could have an easier time catching violent criminals who are mentally ill and juries might be more willing to convict mentally ill defendants than others. In addition; judges might be more inclined to sentence mentally ill violent offenders to prison than other violent offenders. The reasons why the total number of mentally ill ended up behind bars are not clear. One thought is that the release of the 'warehousing' of the mentally ill in the 1970s may have shifted patients from mental institutions to prisons. Ditton also noted that homelessness was more than double among mentally ill inmates than among others. For example, for mentally ill inmates, 20 percent of those in state prisons and 30 percent of those in jails were homeless the year before imprisonment. Compare those figures to 9 percent of the other inmates in state prisons and 17 percent of the other inmates in jails.

Random Violence and Managed Health Care

Lonnie Davis, a 22-year-old from Seattle, Washington went on a killing spree May 29, 1999. Davis had previous run-ins with the law in King County, but he had no known history of violence or a known history of mental illness, as reported by the Associated Press. The rampage started with Davis stabbing his mother (age 46), his sister's son (18 months), with a three-inch pairing knife about 10:00 or 11:00 A.M. Davis changed his clothes and left the house. About 1:30 P.M. he swerved his mother's car into a motorcycle on Interstate 5 in Shoreline. The motorcyclist had to have a leg amputated below the knee. Although Davis' car was totaled and burned, he escaped on foot. Moments later a woman (age 63) was found in a pool of blood with a post-hole digger next to her. Davis then attacked another woman in her yard and hit her with an object that broke her neck, critically injuring her. He then found a house with weapons and starting firing at officials, causing Deputy Diana Russell to be hit in the head by flying glass and ricocheting bullets. Davis was eventually killed with a sniper's bullet.

One would have to ask "What stimulated such random anger and who was the object of the anger?" Why was it so haphazardly displaced toward anyone who appeared in his path? Clearly, guns were not the medium of the anger – Davis was! A warped state of mind found the path of least resistance to expel the anger. Was it an internal problem with too much impulsiveness, or too little self-control? Was it an external problem with too much environmental pressure or unacceptable abilities for dealing with environmental pressures? We believe that it was an internal problem with very little self-control. A history could easily confirm this hypothesis. Obviously, the lost of control and the need for power can follow many routes and take many forms. Much has to be identified early and altered in a person like Davis before he can hope to escape from violent acts because he simply lost control or, as some news media like to say, "he snapped." That "snap" has been sitting and waiting to happen for a long time and would have been observable by a mental health professional as something other than the potential to "snap." The use of the so-called "snap theory" is simply a way to avoid the problem.

The result of violence generally does not make any difference if the perpetrator is psychotic, psychopathic, a person with a grudge, a terrorist, a gang member or anyone else. However, laws governing mental illness can be a block to treatment. For instance the 'right to refuse treatment,' including not renewing psychotropic prescriptions can lead to disastrous consequences and need to be re-examined.

Mental illness affects 20 percent of the U.S. population and treatment costs at least $67 billion a year, according to a 1997 study for the U.S. Department of Health and Human Services. However, spending on mental treatment has been slashed due to America's managed health care revolution. A May report by the Hay Group consulting firm, commissioned by mental health advocates, found mental health spending fell 54 percent in the decade 1988-1997. Spending on all health care declined only 7 percent, as reported by John Hendren in the Lawrence Journal World on August 10, 1998. What impact does this cutback on treatment have on violence?

Unfortunately, the choice of treatment for dangerous individuals is no longer left up to the professionals best able to assess their need for treatment. Instead, treatment must be approved by managed health care, even when the patient is willing to receive the treatment and in cases where it is needed immediately. This is a serious problem in the health care system. This suggests that mental health problems, such as violence, would be more common in the future. The reason is that it is so difficult for patients to obtain proper treatment when needed without having to go through several branching telephone stations and answering several questions about insurance. An exercise not appreciated when experiencing severe mental problems with a short temper.

It does not make sense for a competent, licensed professional to have to obtain 'prior approval' to treat someone in a crisis. This is especially true when the managed health care case manager has no sense of the level of emergency and frequently does not have the training or experience to deal with the problem. This authority, as well as the liability, should belong to the provider – not just the liability alone. Our prediction is that emotional problems will become more severe in the future since the route to the mental health care provider is increasingly fraught with obstacles that are more business oriented than health care oriented.

LAW ENFORCEMENT EMPLOYEES

A total of 13,052 city, county, and state police agencies submitting Uniform Crime Reporting data reported collectively that they employed 586,756 officers and 226,780 civilians in 1995. The National average rate of 2.4 full-time officers for every 1,000 inhabitants in 1995 showed a slight increase from the 1994 figure, 2.3 per 1,000 inhabitants. Geographically, the highest rate of officers to population was recorded in the Northeastern States where there were 2.7 officers per 1,000 inhabitants. With increases in funding these ratios are expected to improve in the future.

THE EFFECT OF THE MIRANDA DECISION

The statistics on crime clearance rates (solving crimes) shows a marked decline in the years following the Miranda decision, according to Mona Charen, as reported in her column of October 7, 1998. In 1963, a 23-year-old man with a prior arrest record and an eighth grade education was arrested by the Phoenix police for questioning in the kidnapping and rape of an 18-year-old woman. At the close of two hours of interrogation, Ernesto Miranda orally confessed to the crime, described the rape, and signed a statement certifying that the confession was voluntary. He also indicated that no threats or intimidation had been used, and that he fully understood his rights. He was tried, convicted, and sentenced to 20 years in prison. He appealed his conviction because his attorney had not been present during questioning, therefore his confession could not be treated as truly voluntary. The Supreme Court agreed and in 1965 issued one of the most famous criminal decisions in history, Miranda vs. Arizona.

The **Miranda rights** are: (1) "You have the right to remain silent. (2) Anything you say can be used against you in a court. (3) You have the right to talk to a lawyer for advice before we ask you any questions and to have your lawyer with you during questioning. (4) If you cannot afford a lawyer and want one before we ask you any questions, one will be appointed. (5) If you decide to answer questions now without a lawyer present, you still have the right to stop answering at any time until you talk to a lawyer. Do you understand these rights? Are you willing to waive your rights and talk to us?"

Miranda was re-tried and convicted. He was paroled in 1972 and was killed in a bar fight. The crime was never solved. Critics warned that the decision would make it more difficult for police to solve crimes. About 30 years later, the National Center for Policy Analysis issued a report by Professor Paul G. Cassell of the University of Utah College of Law. He argued that the Miranda Rights hampered the ability of the police to solve crimes, resulting in significant percentages of criminals going unpunished. The violent-crime-solving rate before 1960 was about 60 percent. By 1968, it had dropped to 47 percent. According to Cassell, there were between 56,000 and 136,000 more unsolved and unpunished violent crimes in 1995 because of the Miranda decision. Miranda rights have had the effect of discouraging potential defendants – even those guilty and stricken with conscience or too scared to lie – from confessing the truth. Consequently, more lawyers are brought in to argue the case and heavier court costs ensue. More jurors feel intimidated by the process and more citizens feel the justice system is flawed.

---

[8] U.S. Department of Justice, Federal Bureau of Investigation. Released October 13, 1996 by the FBI National Press Office, Washington, D.C. (Http://www.fbi.gov/ucr/ucr95prs.htm).

[9] Bachman, R. 1994. *Violence against women: A national crime victimization survey report*, U.S. Department of Justice Bureau of Justice Statistics. January, 1.

[10] Astor, R.A. and Behre, W.J. 1997. Violent and nonviolent children's and parents' reasoning about family and peer violence, *Behavioral Disorders*, Vol. 22, 4, 231-245.

[11] Tiffany, D.W. and Shontz, F.C. 1963. Fantasized Danger as a Function of Parent-Child Controlling Practices, *Journal of Consulting Psychology*, 27, 3, 278. The authors found that emotionally disturbed children, who had exhibited anger, experienced more environmental pressure than nonpsychiatric children.

[12] Fremouw, W.J., Westrup, D., and Pennypacker, J. 1997. Stalking on campus: The prevalence and strategies for coping with stalking. *Journal of Forensic Sciences*, 42, 4, 666-669.

Chapter 3: The Illusion Of Reality

Gaining control, and staying in control in a responsible way, may seem to be an impossible task, but it is not. Many individuals do it every day for a lifetime of good mental health.[13] Early theorists/researchers such as Bettelheim and Janowitz (1950)[14] examined the Dynamics of prejudice from a more ideological frame of ethnic intolerance and group hostility within the psychoanalytic point of view. We want to broaden this perspective by examining all control problems within the framework of sensation and perception and include our interpretation of later theorists/researchers such as Harry Helson, Ph.D.[15] and Fritz Heider, Ph.D.[16]

Psychologists, biologists, physiologists, and sociologists have used variations of Harry Helson's concept of Adaptation Level, as an adjustment to environmental conditions, for decades. Adaptation level is affected by the reaction of an individual to stimulation, as well as by action of stimulation upon the individual. For every situation confronting an individual there is established an adaptation level that is an interaction between the focal, contextual (background), and residual or past stimuli. These three sources of experience combine to equal the total experience for an individual, who then brings this experience to all new situations.

Fritz Heider, a contemporary to Harry Helson, added another dimension to our understanding of experience by altering the effect of the focal stimulus. Heider's theory denoted the level of cognitive dissonance balance in everything we perceived. Thus, an alteration of the 'intended' stimulus, in Helson's view, left us with a new experience. For example, look at the following logic of one person perceiving another person.

A perceives B and, let us say, A likes B. Therefore there is a positive relationship between A and B. Let us also assume that A recently learned that B possessed characteristic, C, that A did not like.

Therefore, A likes B but does not like the characteristic that B possesses, that is, C. Incidentally, B and C are considered a Unit Formation since they are assumed to go together. These relationships look like Figure 3.

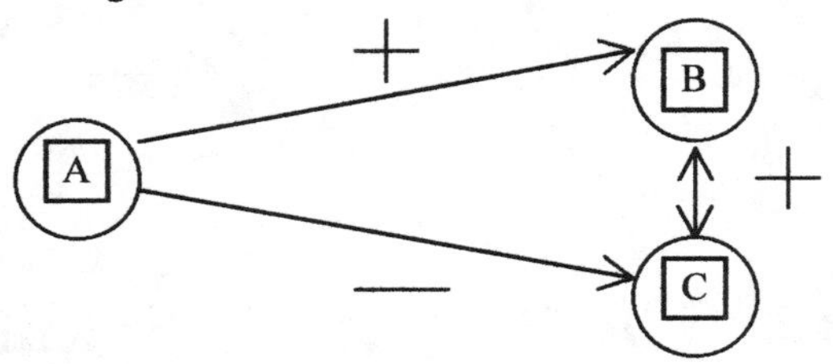

FIGURE 3. HEIDER'S COGNITIVE DISSONANCE MODEL.

In the above diagram, A perceives B. This perception is experienced as a positive relationship. B possesses trait C, which A perceives as negative. Lastly, B and C go together and must be considered as such by A. The negative between A and C causes this relationship to be imbalanced. The perception must have all pluses to be balanced. How does a person handle this imbalanced relationship causing cognitive dissonance? (1) A can tell B that he must disown characteristic C (e.g., controlling behavior) for them to remain friends and, therefore, the B to C plus sign becomes a minus sign, which is a balance. (2) A can accept C (the friend's controlling behavior) which then becomes a plus perception and, therefore, balanced. (3) A can reject B with a minus and not be bothered with the cognitive dissonance any longer. As long as only one negative sign exists, an imbalance will cause dissonance.

The first step in understanding control is to recognize that it differentiates between what we experience and what "really" occurs. For example, in the above example is the person perceived as overly controlling or are we too passive? Understanding our experience (true awareness of one's self in terms of feelings, sensations, beliefs and goals) gives us increased feelings of control. Understanding our experienced control[17], that is, the control we feel, may be even more of a determiner of our actions than the control that actually exists. Some times, we accomplish things we never thought we had the power or control to do. No one has ever predicted or explained the hero in wartime or in other crises. Heroes just surface at the proper time and do what is expected of them.

We intend to show that the experience of control is crucial not only to our psychological well being, but to our physical health and other people's physical health as well.[18] First, let us talk about what we think we perceive. Life is full of illusions. One we have all seen some time in our life is the Müller-Lyer Illusion, which is the following Figure 4.

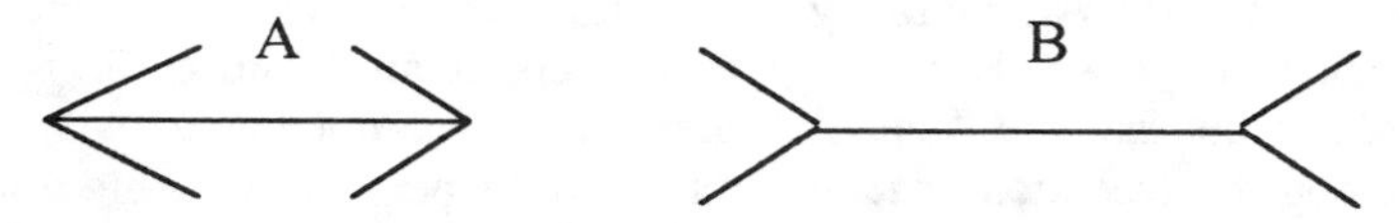

FIGURE 4. THE MÜLLER-LYER ILLUSION.

The question asked, is "which horizontal line is the longest, A or B." The great majority of respondents say B, when in fact both lines are the same length. This illusion is a simple physical stimulus. However, most stimuli we encounter that cause problems for us, are social. A social stimulus is far more complicated than the simple physical stimulus seen above.

EXPERIENCE DOES NOT (ALWAYS) EQUAL REALITY

EXPERIENCED CONTROL THEORY

With the above perspectives of Heider and Helson and the concept of illusions behind us, let us explore the experience of control. Experienced Control Theory is the result of thirty-five years of clinical practice, teaching, research, and observations. Our work includes males and females of all ages and racial groups. They come from a variety of cultures and geographic areas, and from a broad array of human conditions and events. Some individuals have had very serious control problems (from hostility against others to hostility against self), on a national level, with groups, and on an individual scale. Some of these problems have been acute, others chronic and serial. Some individuals have expressed these problems because of situations, some are enduring personality problems, and some are both. We want to discuss some of them to help in the understanding of when and where different kinds of control are useful or harmful.

Our goal is to help find ways of identifying alternatives to anger, whether directed at others or us. We want to help identify strengths, weaknesses, and ways to change and make life more adaptable and possibly contribute to altering problems by a more complete understanding of control problems.

First, let us examine an important aspect of our experiences. This has to do with perception, which as we use here is a combination of our personal history and what we actually experience. For example, when we were young, we were taught that reality, not our experience of it, was what counted. We learned to compare what we felt to be objective measures to our experiences. We used a thermometer, scale, ruler, or rain gauge to find out what was "correct" and, when it did not agree with us, we told ourselves that we did not really experience what we thought we did. Alternatively, we sometimes like to think that the instrument is wrong. However, we now talk about "wind chill," since we recognize that the "actual" temperature does not tell us what the sensation or perception of temperature is to us personally. Some times, we do not use a ruler to decorate a room. Instead, we use our "artistic talents" to place an object in the most "artful" place, even if it does measure closer to one wall than the other. Obviously, personal perception works better for us in some ways than the actual physical stimulus.

Some of us remember when we complained of feeling sick. Mom, Dad, or someone, caring for us usually felt our forehead with the back of their hand or took our temperature with a thermometer. If our temperature was higher than normal, we stayed home from school. However, if our temperature was normal, off we went, perhaps still feeling some discomfort or pain.

Faking an illness to avoid threatening events such as the old stomachache ploy on the day of the math test does not teach us to cope. Neither do consistent misperceptions such as prejudices or biases, which are learned. Rather, such distorted learning teaches us to prolong pain and increase biases. These are not good behaviors to learn, but rarely do we have the accurate measure (physical or social) to teach us what is the most correct and appropriate. However, feeling a physical illness or psychological pain in the face of threatening events can be very real and very painful, even when the problem cannot be objectively measured. No fever, no redness, no swelling, nothing Mom or Dad, or the doctor can find, so we are told "it must be in your head." We learn to be suspicious of the world of subjective experience inside ourselves, even reject it altogether. In contrast, we learn to believe it regardless of objectivity, despite its constant presence and frequent pain. The expression, "it must be in your head" is a put-down that misses the mark in understanding the problem. Many murders take place because the problems were "only" in the head of the murderer. Should they be ignored, too? Of course not! We know that what is in our head can do great things for the world or incur irreparable damage to things and people.

Do we ever check the thermostat before we put on a sweater, and when the temperature is "normal," tell ourselves we are not cold? On another day, when the temperature is the same, we feel warm! Alternatively, we look at the clock when our stomach growls and, if it is not time for lunch, tell ourselves we are not hungry. Yet we continue to feel warm or hungry, and the conflict between what we perceive and what objective measures indicate we should perceive make us upset and frustrated. We express frustration as a lack of control and we gain control by changing the thermostat or by eating something. This simple form of getting in control happens every day.

The Goodness Of Fit: How Realistic Is It?

The similarity between what we experience and what "really" exists is sometimes called the "goodness of fit," whether it is physical or social stimuli. Imagine that there was a way to measure the quality of an evening out with friends. As my wife and I are driving with friends along a familiar but dark highway, it begins to rain. We are comfortable and enjoying the prospect of a needed rain helping our garden. When we arrive at our destination we are surprised to hear one friend say how hard the rain came down, and he stated with conviction that, "at least an inch" of rain had fallen in a matter of minutes. The other friend expressed great concern about the sharp lightening. She believed it the "most severe" she had ever seen. We realized that the country drive had been unfamiliar and in a different context, and threatening to our friends. Later that evening the local weather report indicated that less than a half inch of rain had fallen throughout the evening and made no mention of the lightening. Our experience was confirmed. Not too much rain, not too much lightening, but nice, refreshing rain for the garden. We are impressed how four people seemingly experience the same thing, yet perceive it so differently.

Some individuals strive to increase the goodness of fit, the similarity between our perception or experience and reality. That is a remarkable goal but it is rarely a perfect match. The friend who thought there was much heavier rain may be very uncomfortable driving on wet highways because of having experienced an accident under such conditions. The friend concerned with the lighting may have grown up hearing stories of the great lightening strikes that burned down grandpa's barn. Unless we know someone extremely well, we may never understand the experiences that drive their understandings and perceptions of mild or severe events. We may not understand our own. For example, suppose a line was drawn on the wall and 100 carpenters were asked how long it is. These responses would fit perfectly in the following curve shown in Figure 5 below, which is a normal distribution. About 68 of the carpenters' responses will appear in the middle of the normal curve around the actual number, but they will not be accurate. Some will be too long and some will be too short. Few if any will get it right. This is considered a normal bell curve as illustrated below.

Another way to examine the curve is to use school grades. For example, put a "C" in the middle where 68% of the individuals are. To the right at the next vertical line put a "B," and then at the next vertical line put an "A" for individuals who were the closest in getting the number right. The lower grades are to the left of the "C." We rarely perceive a physical stimulus accurately, unless highly trained to do so. Moreover, physical stimuli are the easiest to perceive when compared to social stimuli. Greater mistakes occur with social or interpersonal stimuli. Most of us fall in the "C" range, which accounts for many interpersonal errors and conflicts reflecting control problems.

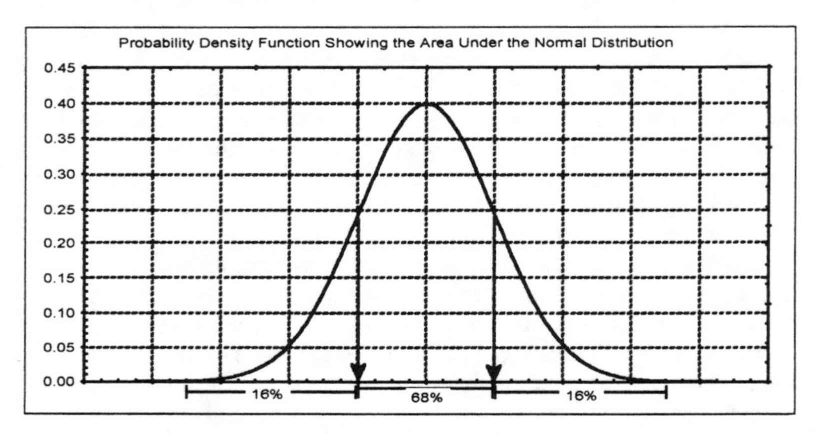

FIGURE 5. NORMAL DISTRIBUTION OF THE WAY WE PERCEIVE.

IMPROVING THE GOODNESS OF FIT

With education and experience, we can learn to improve the goodness of fit and move closer to the middle of the normal distribution. It does not take special talent, only a desire to understand our environment and ourselves the best we can. If we do not make that effort, we will continue to misperceive and to make inappropriate choices and responses. Our friend with a poor goodness of fit perception for lightening strikes may live in fear of every storm. The friend who thought the rain was coming down much heavier than it was, might choose to stay home to avoid what are perceived as relatively unsafe highways, denying himself pleasure and opportunities. Alternatively, we may underestimate the danger of a storm and find ourselves on highways that are not safe when we think they are. We may try to convince our friends we are right and lose their friendship because we do not take into account the depth and reasons for their experiences.

Perceptions are not always the way that they seem. We must learn to question our own perceptions until we become comfortable with them. They will never be the same as other people's perceptions. These differences are what make us interesting to each other, and sometimes difficult. Different people perceive illusions in different ways, even as simple as they may be. Just think how complicated social stimuli are and how much they open us up to mistakes in a single conversation! On the positive side, just think how this same fact of different percepts gives us a variety of experiences and differences in art. Sometimes it creates serious problems such as three people standing on the same street corner witnessing a car accident. It is difficult for the police to believe that the three observers were all on the same corner at the same time when they compare their accounts of the accident.

Ignoring reality altogether is the other extreme. Beliefs that our water is poisoned or that the boss is a hatchet murderer present their own kinds of problems. Most of us live somewhere in the middle. Most of us experience events every day and we accept most of them as they appear. Alternatively, we add our own spin, perhaps not consciously or deliberately, to fit the notions we have about others and ourselves. These notions may be positive or negative, but most of the time they lack merit and reflect our own experiences, beliefs, values, roles, likes and dislikes. We have not thought them through completely. Maybe someone else's concerns or opinions influence us or we have unrecognized desires that their notions satisfy.

For example, your husband appears to enjoy the company of members of the opposite sex, particularly with a woman you dislike. You conclude that your spouse is being too friendly. Your best friend listens to your concerns and says nothing to convince you otherwise. After all, your best friend, whose husband had an affair, was just divorced. Therefore, your friend convinces you that your marriage is in trouble. This could be a misperception of social stimuli, as conditioned by your friend's background, which could lead to many misdirected problems and decisions.

Imagine the difference if your friend had suggested that your husband is not interested in replacing you, but is still attracted to the same qualities that sparked feelings for you. He saw you as good looking, humorous, and full of energy. Such counsel might induce thoughts about if and how you have changed since your courtship. Maybe you are not the same person your spouse married or perhaps he simply admires those qualities in others and you have just noticed that aspect of his behavior. Perhaps you need to refurbish some of those qualities. Alternatively, maybe you have not changed. In either event, your friend's comments could help you focus on the real issues and take corrective actions, rather than waste time and energy on unfounded worries. However, remember that your friend's view is based on her experience, not on yours! Furthermore, she is probably not a professional counselor.

USING EXPERIENCE TO FEEL IN CONTROL

Imagine that your boss passes you in the hall without speaking. You perceive him to be angry with you and displeased with your work. You react to him as if your perceptions are fact – a little like an optical illusion, only this is a social perception. Your perception, in turn, affects your response to him, and therefore his response to you. It even gets more complex, particularly when it goes on for a long time. In truth, your boss may have a headache or have shot a terrible round of golf. However, days of discomfort pass before you clear things up, days in which you feel that your relationship, maybe even your job is out of your control. How many times have people wasted energy this way or even loss their temper and became aggressive?

You can and should talk to your boss about your perceptions. That is a constructive use of your experience and will usually bring greater rapport. However, in other situations, you may feel that there is no one to talk to, no way of expressing your feelings, no way of "clearing things up." Imagine that your rival gets the promotion you felt you deserved. Do you talk to your boss? Probably not. You probably avoid your rival and you might even sabotage that person's effort to succeed. Your behavior will change in some way, and those who observe it, including yourself, may not understand the cause of the change. You make plans to change jobs. You may find yourself acting meaner than you had ever thought possible. "What's wrong with me?" you ask. "I must be losing control!" You are not using your experiences appropriately here; your experience is using you!

Look at another example. Imagine fishing from the bank of a creek. The sun is shining and the air is warm, but you are sitting in the shade of an old oak tree, and the breeze is cool. If someone asked whether you felt in control of your environment or controlled by the environment, you would probably say, "I feel in control here."

Now, imagine that a storm comes up. The sky darkens, the wind blows, and cold rain pelts down. You lean into the wind to make your way to your car. Shielding your eyes you get in the car, dripping wet, without a single fish, with torrents of rain rolling down your windshield. You would claim little, if any, experienced control over that situation.

Let us return to the sunny scene and imagine that catching fish was important, critical, in fact. Your wife likes to tease you about the energy you put into fishing and you were determined to catch a fish this time, just to show some reward for your time. How much control do you feel when the fish do not bite, even on a beautiful day. Finally, you rationalize that you are collecting a few hours of relaxation for yourself, even if you are caught in a downpour.

The week was hectic. The deadlines have been met and you feel a strong need to spend time by yourself. Two days lie ahead, during which you do not have to do dishes or laundry. Just as you settle down, feet up, TV tray in hand, your favorite CD playing, the doorbell rings. Your best old college friend drove by with her family and remembered that you lived here. Your sense of control over the upcoming weekend whizzed right out the door the minute you swung it open. However, stop and think for a minute. Your first option was to not open the door. Nevertheless, you did! You still have many control options. You can set the boundaries for how much time you really want to spend with your friend. Your can decide if they are staying with you or at a motel. You can tell them the best places for them to go out to eat without obligating yourself. The extent of obligation is up to you. The first question is, do you really want to spend some time with your friend and her family? It could turn out to be the best weekend you have had in a long time. Sometimes, having control is simply to appreciate and enjoy going along with an event as it occurs.

What we will come to understand is the following; the amount of control we feel in a given situation may not always be the amount of control we actually have. What is important is the difference between the amount of control we feel we have, the amount of control we actually have, and the amount of control we want to have. Think about greeting unexpected friends at the door. We still have a lot more control than the situation at first appears. Do we want control badly enough to find it and use it? Learn the difference between desiring and gaining control over the events in your life and over yourself. Understanding that difference allows us to cope better with events and with our reactions to events and to other people. Learning the disparity between desiring and actually gaining control will help us diagnose those times when we feel bothered by something, but do not know what or why. It will help us respond most effectively to situations in which we feel stress. It can also help us achieve our goals. As we will see, control is essential to achievement. Those who experience themselves as lacking control, often behave as if they actually lacked control. They do not make choices, 'stand up' for their beliefs or desires, or act to direct their lives. Conversely, those who realistically experience themselves as being in control, behave as if they are, and achieve what they desire. A person who complaints about the government but does not vote is a person who not only perceives that they have no control, but does not choose to exercise any control. Remember that we act according to our experience of control, not according to the control that actually exits.[19] Being in control begets control. Build it, and control will come.

Four Sources of Control

The research literature shows that experienced control comes from four sources. They are represented with the Figure 6 image of a LIFE PRESERVER.

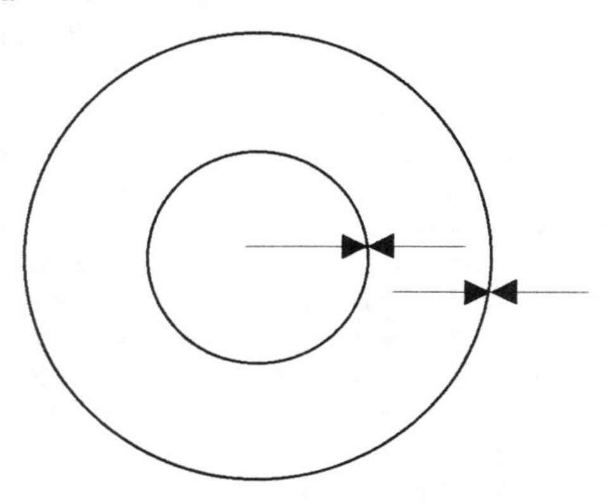

FIGURE 6. FOUR DIFFERENT KINDS OF CONTROL.

1. When we are in the center of our control model or LIFE PRESERVER, we experience impulses *from* inside ourselves, such as hunger, fatigue, or rage. These impulses are CFI, for impulses *from* Internal.
2. The arrow pointing against CFI of the LIFE PRESERVER represents control *over* internal impulses (COI), such as control over appetite or anger. These we call COI for self-control or control *over* Internal.
3. The inside arrow directed toward the outer edge of the LIFE PRESERVER represents control *over* the environment (COE), such as taking shelter in a rainstorm. This is our competence, mastery, or control *over* External (environment) or COE.
4. The world outside the LIFE PRESERVER symbolized by the arrow external to the LIFE PRESERVER represents pressures *from the environment* (CFE), such as weather, bosses or

demanding jobs, angry spouses, violent people, wars, etc. These are called CFE or control *from* External (environment).

Let us consider this idea of staying afloat in a LIFE PRESERVER in the sea of our environment. In the center of the LIFE PRESERVER, we are feeling many different impulses from inside (CFI), both physical and emotional, such as fatigue, hunger, sexual desire, anger, pain, etc. We exercise control over these impulses to one degree or another by using self-control. We use control OI to determine whether it is appropriate for us to fix a snack or resist eating, express our happiness by daydreaming and whistling cheerfully, or 'buckle down' and concentrate on our work. In addition, we exert varying degrees of control over pressures from the environment by using control OE. For example, we turn on the lights or go to bed when it gets dark. On the other hand, we may open our umbrella or let ourselves get soaked when it rains. Lastly, we can break the speed law by running a red light and taking chances or be cautious by stopping. We experience such pressures as darkness, rain, speed laws, parental discipline, spouse's nagging, and the boss's silence, as forces from the environment (CFE). Our physical and emotional self is inside the LIFE PRESERVER; the environment is outside. The LIFE PRESERVER, control COI, and COE, helps us cope with both ourselves and the 'sea' in which we float. An arrow represents each force. In Figure 6 in the above illustration, the arrows are approximately equal in length suggesting equal amounts of control. Actually, the four controls continuously vary with each other with every changing thought, feeling, situation, and perception. They are in constant flux throughout the day and throughout our lives.

LEVELS OF CONTROL

We experience all four sources of control at the same time all the time – the configuration of the four controls varies with each experience. Examining less than the four sources of control at the same time makes as much sense as a racehorse that has less than four legs competing in the Kentucky Derby. For example, how much sense does it make to know someone's level of self-control without also knowing their level of impulsiveness, or environmental control, or level of control over the environment. It does not make sense to study one type of control without the other three, however, many studies of control examine one, two, or three of the control components without looking at the effects of the remaining control components. Such studies are, at best, suggestive, and generally are worthless! Control problems cannot be broken down into a single measure unless all four-control components are included in some statistical way. Understanding control problems requires the recognition of the interaction effect of many aspects of control. The control picture cannot be subdivided into smaller elements that are examined without respect to the whole picture – the other control components.

Not only do we need to understand the four control components, but also we need to understand that the four control components rapidly change to fit changing situations. Consequently, the arrows representing each force change in weight with each changing moment. A heavy arrow indicates high control. A thin arrow indicates little control. When we feel more pressure from internal impulses than we feel over those impulses, the arrows take the form shown in Figure 7.

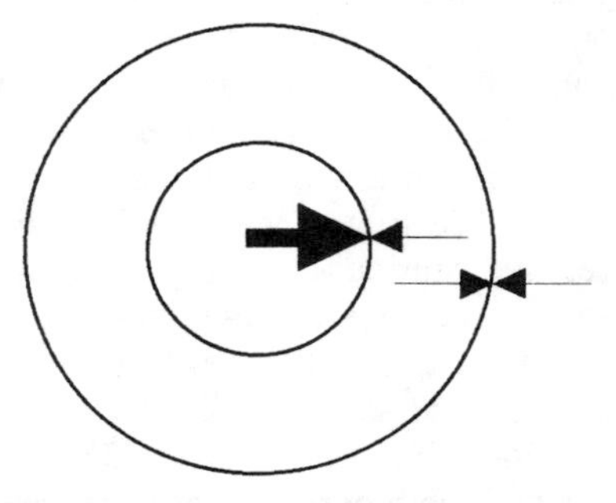

FIGURE 7. HIGH CONTROL FROM INTERNAL (CFI).

In contrast to the Internal Locus, when we feel more pressure from the environment than over it, the heavy arrow would appear as in Figure 8. This would indicate very high pressures from the environment such as overwhelming demands from someone, bad weather, violence, or anything that we perceived as overpowering.

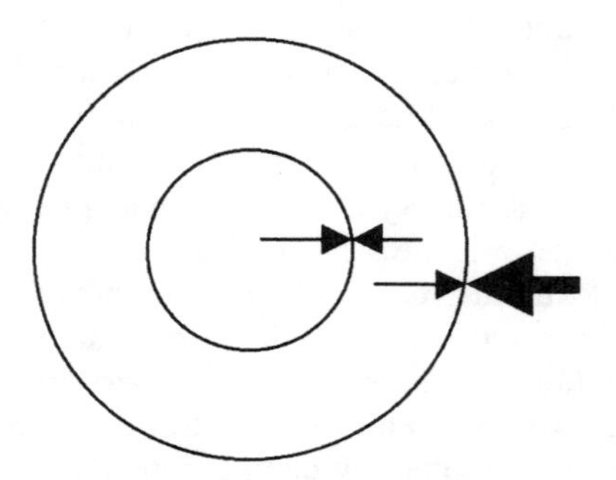

FIGURE 8. HIGH CONTROL FROM THE ENVIRONMENT (CFE).

Because environmental pressures and responses to them change constantly, our experience of control could look like each of these illustrations in the space of a single day or, for that matter, an hour or less. In addition, it could look like Figure 9, such as having a "sense of control," which is appropriate in most situations. COI plus COE equals Self-Direction, which is being in control at both loci. CFI plus CFE equals NonSelf-Direction, which is being out of control at both loci. More is said about Self-Direction and NonSelf-Directed later.

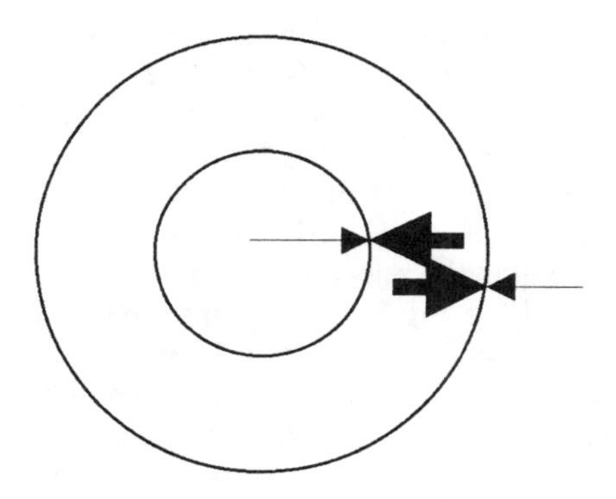

FIGURE 9. SELF-DIRECTED CONTROL.

THE ENVIRONMENT: MANY OVERLAPPING ELEMENTS!

So far, we have talked about "the environment" as if it were a single consistent part of our life. In reality, we function in a combination of parts of many different environments. For example, some writers are questioning the influence of parenting on children, particularly in the wake of the Columbine High School shootings. What is the influence of the "Home" and "Parental" context in rearing a child. James Garbarino of Cornell University, author of "Lost Boys: Why Our Sons Turn Violent And What We Can Do About Them," raises an important and practical point for established psychology. He writes, "What's been under appreciated, underdiscussed, is the role of context, peers being a subcategory." Our research is inextricably linked to the effects of context on behavior, which is discussed in detail in Chapter 5.

Some environments are relatively self-contained and separate from other environments. "Work" and "School" are very different environments for many people, but can run over into the home environment. For most people, they remain separate. Other environmental pressures are external forces that come into play in a variety of physical settings. "Other people," for example, affect us in many environments. Consequently, in talking about control, it is useful to segment "the environment" into various kinds of situations or contexts. We have identified seven Standard situations known to almost everyone at some time during their life. Many of us function in several each day and shift back and forth frequently. First, each of us has or had a "Home" of some kind. Even if we live alone, the place where we live with our cat, our bird or with only our favorite things is our "Home" and immediate family. At times, our family includes a number of "Other People," depending on how many relatives are available to us.

"School" or a learning situation is another context with which nearly everyone has some experience. Some have only bad memories. Others have very good memories. School includes parts of many other environments. Other situations include "Other people" in "General," the "Same Sex," and the "Opposite Sex." Think of ourselves as working parents and we will add situations of "Work" and "Community." The Community may mean church, the supermarket, the dentist, driving to work, going shopping, the neighborhood, or the speed limit in a school zone. "Community" usually means what we define it to mean. If we live in a rural area, it frequently means the whole town. If we live in a city, the community may be more constricted. Some people see the neighborhood as their community, while other people see the country as the community. The Chamber of Commerce of a city sees the whole city as the community, while gang members see only a limited territory as their community. Our perceptions depend on our experiences and our desires.

The experience of a situation changes according to the presence or absence of "Other People" or various elements in the situation. For example, our comments to a girlfriend change when her mother walks in the room. When our context is in constant flux so is our perception of it. Our perception changes as a function of the change in the situation, thereby causing the four control components to change and thus, our experience and balance of control is changed.

The situation, "Other People," of course represents everyone from our mother-in-law to the mail carrier. Sometimes we perceive these as members of the "Same Sex" or "Opposite Sex," sometimes just as other people that are not necessarily peers.

Some situations may be more relevant for some people than for others. For example, "Work" may be inappropriate for a young child who does not have a job, while "Hospital" may be appropriate for a patient who is mentally or physically ill. No two people will perceive the same things in the same situation. Part of what we perceive comes from our experiences. That difference is how we perceive and act differently to the same stimulus conditions.[20] In psychology, this is referred to as Validity Generalization that fails to be included in many psychological tests. Even industry is ahead of psychology in this regard. For example, if a manufacturer is producing a car chair for children for use in and out of a car, they will test it in many different situations. They want to show that the validity of their assertions meets all conditions or situations. Psychometrics should do the same thing. It is a well-known fact that the context alters the individual's experience. That is why we count on winning at the "home game," the context is different than when the team plays "away."

MEASURING OUR FEELINGS OF CONTROL

By using the four components or sources of control (CFI, COI, COE, CFE), we can show how much of the four types of control we feel in each of the above situations or any other situation we can imagine. By comparing two opposing control responses for a situation at different times, we can compare our feelings at different times – in different situations. This can be accomplished with the standard situations or special situations we choose from our work setting (sales, accounting, secretarial, etc), and measure different situations than the Standard situations provided in the Tiffany Control Scales. For example, people on the West Coast appear to have a greater tolerance for earthquakes than Midwesterners. Midwesterners seem to have a better tolerance for tornadoes than Westerners. People on the East Coast have a better tolerance for Hurricanes than Westerners or Midwesterners. These differences could be measured to determine the level of experienced control for any of these natural events to determine how they differ by location. These findings would help determine if location adds to our experience of control, that is, our stress and low coping ability. Another measure of the feelings of control is in the process of parenting, particularly when things go awry.

Ann, a working mother, held a responsible job as Executive Secretary for a large legal corporation. She experienced the four components in many situations daily. Her problem was to assume an attitude that her "latch-key children" would learn to care for themselves after they got out of school and before she returned home each day. She was less then two hours behind them, but the two children, daughter age 13 and son age 17, still needed some training in self-care and learning to be responsibly independent.

Mark Twain's dicta that children at age 13 should be buried and then dug up at age 24 would be one solution, but not for Ann. She loved her children and wanted them to learn to be able to care for themselves. She maintained that she was responsible for the children. However, she failed to follow through on discipline or sometimes even administer discipline out of her guilt for not being home when the kids got out of school. In addition, she did not see this as something her husband should have to share. Consequently, the adolescents did what they generally do in this kind of situation. They begin lying about when they got home; they went places they were told not to go; they even started to come home after mom was home and made up lies about why. Her son was particularly bad about lying. The mother's control FE increased, which subsequently increased control FI, since the two components show a nonlinear correlation of .68. At that stage in the process she started hitting the kids in a rage. The boy hit back and injured his mother. The son did not know external limits from past training and responded as he always had. In addition, COE lashed out at the weak CFE (mother) and finally he overstepped his boundary and mom was injured. The state social service was called in and the son had to be temporarily moved to a group home for boys. The mother felt like a failure and the parents argued about where to place the blame. The story did not have to end this way. Simple administration of consistent discipline would have helped, particularly if efforts had been made to check on the kids to see that they were doing what they were supposed to be doing. Many parents confuse freedom with responsibility. Children want and need structure, although they fight it at times. They should be part of the decision process in establishing rules. Involvement increases with age. Without structure, the parent is relying on animal instincts to guide the children's developmental process. It will not work and never has. Some responsible adult must always be there, perhaps in the background. Remember the "Lord of the Flies." Children, as well as grownups like to expand their area of control. Responsibility has to be part of the training to help us curb a natural tendency – to expand our sphere of control. Sometimes we do it without realizing it. Sometimes it is our only goal in life!

In Chapter 4, we will look more closely at each of the four types of control and the results of experiencing various levels of loss of control. Extreme violence and control does not start with a single incident. Many smaller circumstances prompt bad decisions that lead to an increasing loss of control and, ultimately, a loss of control in the form of violence, abuse, and even murder. Too much or too little control is dangerous.

---

[13] Tiffany, D.W. 1967. Mental Health: A Function of Experienced Control. *Journal of Clinical Psychology*, 23, 3, 311-315.

[14] Bettelheim, B. and Janowitz, M. 1950. Dynamics of prejudice; A psychological & sociological study of veterans. New York: Harper & Bros.

[15] Helson, H. 1964. *Adaptation-level theory*. . New York: Harper & Bros.

[16] Heider, F. 1958. *The psychology of interpersonal relations*. John Wiley & Sons, New York.

[17] Tiffany, D.W. and Shontz, F.C. 1962. The Measurement of Experienced Control in Pre-adolescents, *Journal of Consulting Psychology*, 26. 6, 491-497.

[18] Steptoe, A. & Appels, A. eds. 1989. *Stress, personal control and health*. New York: John Wiley & Sons.

[19] In scientific literature, inaccurate physical or social perceptions are called *nonveridical* perceptions.

[20] Further reading on situational specificity or validity generalization may be found in the following two references. Tiffany, D.W. and Tiffany, P.G. 1996. Contextual effects on adolescent disorders relevant to coping, *Psychological Reports*, 78, 593-594 and Tiffany, D.W. and Tiffany, P.G. 1999. Overgeneralization of validity generalization in personality inventories: applied issues in testing, *Psychological Reports*, 84, 593-609.

Chapter 4: Control Dynamics

Feeling in control means feeling the amount of control we want to feel from ourselves and the environment and over ourselves and the environment. In this chapter, we will build on the sources of control discussed in Chapter 3 and examine the relationships among them. Our concern in this volume is to present the tools for designing programs wherever there is a concern about control problems. As the reader will learn, control problems are associated with life conditions or situations that make up an individual's circumstances. They are not genetic, but learned behaviors that are determined by the way we perceive our environments. The kind of program for communities, schools, law enforcement, and families depends upon the nature of the problems. We present the tools to design the project and suggest concerns to be covered in the programs designed by individuals who have to deal with the control problems, as they understand them.

The relationships of the four control components shape the situations that cause personal and interpersonal problems. As an example, consider the following case. Joe's wife was growing increasingly distant from Joe. She would not allow him to touch her, would not discuss her feelings with him. She was having an affair with another man. Joe felt completely violated and betrayed (high control CFI and CFE). He loved his wife but felt rejected and abandoned (high control CFI and low control COE) and turned to his oldest daughter for emotional support. The daughter, 16 years old, felt many of the same concerns as Joe. Mom was out of reach for her as well. In Joe's eyes, the daughter took on some of her mother's characteristics by providing the needed emotional support. Soon, daughter and father became very intimate (low control COI), and ultimately became lovers (some release of control CFI for both). However, the daughter soon had second thoughts about the relationship (increasing control COI) and she reported her father to the state Social Services. Sexual abuse was the charge (control CFE), and Joe could not understand how it had gotten started.

INTERNAL CONTROL

CONTROL FROM INSIDE OURSELVES (CFI)

Pressures from within (CFI) determine a lot of how we feel and, ultimately, how we behave. Such pressures may be physiological states, such as hunger, sexual excitement, discomfort, pain, or illness. They may be psychological states, such as anger, despair, delight, or guilt. They can result from environmental pressures (CFEs). For example, we might feel hungry because we are anxious about an upcoming event. We may not connect the hunger and the anxiety. On the other hand, pressures from within ourselves can result from events we consciously and deliberately control. We might feel hunger because we have deliberately fasted for 24 hours. In either case, the response is the same, a high CFI.

Some CFI's are desirable at appropriate times. Sex drive, enthusiasm for one's favorite sports team, or uninhibited joy at seeing an old friend. Anger in some situations may be appropriate CFI's. Most other times high CFI's are not appropriate and need higher self-control or COI's. Some times, we refer to CFI's as a manifestation of 'visceral rage.'

CONTROL OVER INTERNAL IMPULSES (COI)

We control forces inside ourselves (CFI) with self-control over internal impulses (COI). For example, we can control hunger pangs by not thinking about food, by promising ourselves something special later. We can put up with discomfort from physical exercise by believing our clothes will fit again. We can control anger by "holding our temper" and control our impulses by exerting "will-power." We can do this because we have learned the consequences of lashing out at others. We have all cheered the long-suffering hero who, tormented by the bully, finally strikes back. Many times one person may feel they have to be passive and accept abuse by a domineering spouse, an overbearing Mother-in-law, a harassing older sibling, an autocratic boss, or peer. More important than striking back, is when and how to strike back. Exercising control over CFI's takes thought, sensitivity, training, and some COE, which we discuss next. A domineering spouse may be unable or unwilling to change without treatment or leverage, such as the threat of divorce. An overbearing Mother-in-law may only accept our membership in the family after we have successfully challenged her expertise in some way. It is important to know when to be angry. It is more important to figure out the right thing to do about our anger.

EXTERNAL CONTROL

CONTROL OVER THE ENVIRONMENT (COE)

We possess different abilities and skills for exercising control over the environment (COE) that may be a threat to us. Those abilities/skills determine the way we react to the control the environment exerts. If we run into a wall, we can stand there and stare at it or we can climb over it or go around it. If strong winds blow, we can lean into them and keep walking or go indoors. If geographical distance separates us from our friend, we can call or write a letter. When treated unfairly by a police officer, we can argue or file charges. If someone cheats us, we can file a lawsuit. If society sanctions values that we can not accept or expects behavior that violates our sense of freedom or integrity, we can try to change society. We can withdraw and ignore what is going on or we can be angry and bitter but ineffective. In every situation, there are many ways to establish varying levels of control over the environment. To establish appropriate COE, we should thoughtfully look at the options available.

COE is frequently referred to as 'cerebral rage' in contrast with the CFI 'visceral rage.' COE would represent the expression of anger that tends to be thought out before hand or premeditated, while CFI would tend toward rage and impulsivity. The two components combined (CFI plus COE) depict the outward direction of expression of anger which can reflect differential amounts of the two components, thus determining if the expression is more of a visceral or cerebral expression of rage, or an equal combination of the two.

CONTROL FROM THE ENVIRONMENT (CFE)

Pressures from the environment (CFE) become obvious when we talk about control over the environment. These pressures from the environment may be physical objects, such as our opponent in a tennis match. They may be other people, such as police officers, those who are/appear physically stronger, parents, siblings, and members of organizations, such as churches or clubs. They may be abstractions, such as moral restraints, customs, societal values, or politically unfavorable positions. The pressures exerted from environmental pressures vary from slight to strong. CFE's are the most constant and varied of all pressures. They are more distinct than CFI's and in many cases easier to respond to because they are more commonly recognized in our everyday activities and relationships. All kinds of skills, knowledge, power (including weapons, organizations), control, money, and time, are some of the ways of dealing with CFE's.

If we feel we are not able to recognize the pressures from any of these four sources, sit down in a quiet comfortable place and make a list of all the people you talked to yesterday. Now, go back and make a note beside each person, listing your conversation. If that does not start to show you where the CFE pressures are, add another column. In that column, write out what your feelings were (CFI) while talking to each person. Keep adding details to help you understand why and how each of these people caused you to feel pressure.

The next thing to do is organize your list to show the person causing you the greatest pressure. Now you have listed all the pressures you felt from the interpersonal environment yesterday. Do the same thing for each of the other two sources of control – COI and COE. We often deny to ourselves the heavy pressures we encounter daily and therefore, do nothing about them. The pressures become part of our general makeup and all we sense is, "I've got to get away for awhile," rather than, "I know exactly where the pressures come from," and consequently, you now know where to direct your concerns. Let us look at an example of these relationships.

THE FOUR COMPONENTS VIEWED TOGETHER

The following Figure 10 shows the significant difference of the four components for 3608 nonpsychiatric subjects from age 11 to 99 [$F(21,75726)=76.47$; $p<.0001$]. It is readily apparent that the two Self-Directed components are the higher two lines for all situations, while the two NonSelf-Directed components are the two lower lines.

A closer examination of the four components reveals significance extremes for the situation of "Same Sex," and to some extent "Community." For example, both male and female subjects feel more Self-Directed (Self-Control and Competence) in the "Same Sex" situation than they feel NonSelf-Directed (Impulsive and External Control). In contrast, the subjects feel less difference between Self-Direction and NonSelf- Direction in the situations of Work and School. The General situation is added to account for other situations not included in the test. These results are based on the Tiffany Control Scales using the Standard situations.

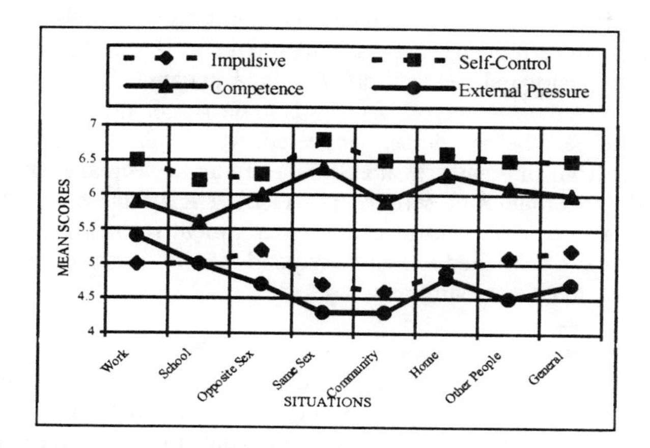

FIGURE 10. THE FOUR COMPONENTS BY SITUATIONS.

RELATIONSHIPS AMONG THE SOURCES OF CONTROL

Control from and over the environment (the solid lines in Figure 10) and from within and over internal impulses (the dashed lines in Figure 10) interact in every situation differently to affect our behavior. Consider the following example of interaction between the control components.

Larry was walking through the woods one crisp, autumn day. The sun shimmered through the trees and their brilliant colors reflected the light. Larry imagined that the worn trail he walked led to a watering hole somewhere, a place known only to Indian maidens and fleet-footed deer.

Without warning, a huge black bear stepped out onto the trail before him. The bear stopped, as if about to charge, and then growled.

Larry's first look at the bear registered substantial pressure from the environment, about as much CFE as one would ever want! His internal response was terror (CFI). His next thought was, "I've got to get hold of myself (COI) before I do something stupid." He quickly assessed his options (COE). He could call for help, but the campsite was too far away for him to be heard. He could climb a tree, but so could the bear. He would have to use the Savage 300 rifle he had slung on his back before he had set out alone. He could try to kill the bear, but he did not want to unless it was necessary. In addition, he was afraid that if he shot and only wounded it, he would just have to deal with an even angrier bear. Perhaps, he could try to frighten it off.

He quickly discharged a thundering round into the path in front of the bear, showering dirt, leaves, and sod in its face. Just as he had hoped, the frightened bear ran off. As it disappeared, the control Larry felt from the environment (CFE) begins to decrease, although not to the level it had been before the bear appeared. At the same time, the control Larry felt from internal pressures (CFI) begins to decrease, and so did his need to maintain high self-control (COI). The alertness he felt while deciding how to gain control of the environment (COE) lingered a bit longer. It too diminished as he relaxed and told his companions back at camp about his electrifying day.

This scene dramatically demonstrates the interplay among the four types of experienced control. Of course, the level of control we experience, regardless of type, is rarely as high as what Larry felt when he came face to face with a bear. Not many of us meet rampaging bears. However, we do meet rampaging bosses, spouses, children, and drivers or customers in a rage, and others who jump in our paths as we walk or drive through different experiences every day.

In the story of the bear, control from the environment plays a major role. In other kinds of situations, other types of control might be dominant. For example, a person with severe illness will feel strong CFI. To some extent, all four types of control are present in every decision we make. We cope best when we can call up the best combination of control types. Take a moment now to think about some of your own experiences. Remember a near miss in an automobile or a quarrel with a parent, colleague, spouse, road rage, customer rage, or a boss's rage. Think about a long-term relationship with a close friend that ended for some reason. How do the four types of control interrelate for each of these events? Remember, to some extent all four control types are present in every situation – one may just stand out more in your memory.

SELF-DIRECTED AND NONSELF-DIRECTED EXPERIENCES

We neither initiate nor develop control CFI and CFE. by definition, they are merely perceptions of the environment or experiences within us. When an experience is NonSelf-Directed, it occurs for reasons outside or beyond us. NonSelf-Directed persons (whose behavior is controlled CFI and CFE), feel at the mercy of events beyond their control. Their behavior is often mechanistic, automatic, passive, and non-responsible. The NonSelf-Directed believe that fate, chance, and powerful others play major roles in their lives. They do not believe they are agents in what happens to them.

Control COI and COE, on the other hand, are in response to maturity, learning, and decision-making. COI and COE are regulation of our self-control and our responses to environmental pressures by personal initiative and choice. Such individuals believe they are agents in what happens to them, such as commitments, responsibilities, intentions, and expectations. Actions COI and COE are generally Self-Directed behaviors, self-actualizing, spontaneous, active, responsible, and creative. Those who display Self-Directed behaviors, for whom control COI and COE predominate, are often called originators, decision-makers, creators, initiators, survivors, leaders – individuals who control their own destinies. They are the people who become CEOs or start their own companies. They are the mothers who decide to form softball teams for their children. They are the grandmothers who open day care centers or write books. They are the people we most admire and frequently follow. In a sample of 3608 nonpsychiatric patients, using a scale from 2 to 20, males and females obtained a Self-Direction score of 12.63 (COI) and 12.39 (COE), respectively. Their NonSelf-Direction scores were 9.63 (CFI) and 9.68 (CFE), respectively. Obviously, Self-Direction is more typical of a normal population for both males and females. Apparently, nonpsychiatric individuals are about 12 percent more Self-Directed than NonSelf-Directed, on the average. This point is discussed more fully later.

All of us are both Self-Directed and NonSelf-Directed in different amounts in different situations. We choose different places and events for each psychological state. Some students believe that schools are there to educate them, so they adopt a passive stance (NonSelf-Direction) and eventually become bored or angry or both and leave. Other students believe that they must participate in their own education. They decide to study longer and harder, complete extra assignments, and stay involved (Self-Direction) in classroom activities. Some women are very passive in the company of men but show real leadership among other women. Some do the reverse. Men can respond to others in much the same way. Which person dominates depends on a number of factors that effect us and that we can change.

Ideally, every person feels in control to the extent that he or she is comfortable with him or herself and others. The educational system could be a perfect vehicle for teaching Self-Direction. Children must be given the opportunity to learn for the sake of learning (COEs). Information and achievement must excite them, to choose what they want to learn and learn because they want to. Instead of giving students the opportunity to learn Self-Direction, the educational system too often is no more than CFE's for managing some individuals. Such a closed system fails as a vehicle for teaching many students to be Self-

Directed at critical times and places in their development. Even more harmful to students and our society is the authority and restriction of the "closed system." Closed and static systems, not open to change, discourage growth in families where parents feel they do not need to teach their children anything beyond what the child learns in school. However, 'home schooling' is on the rise, which clearly opens up the school system and brings family values and change into the curriculum. The jury is still out on how well this change in schooling will work.

Where can we learn Self-Direction, if not at school or home? Most of us teach ourselves through our experiences. One of the great rewards of parenting or teaching is seeing a child turn that corner, where they are able to answer their own dreams for themselves. Unfortunately, most of us, including teachers, have suffered many negative experiences that teach us to be NonSelf-Directed rather than Self-Directed.

WAYS WE LEARN CONTROL

By definition, controls COE and CFE describe interactions with the environment. Sometimes we can change that environment; other times we either can not or choose not to do so. If we feel chilled (CFI) sitting in a cold room (CFE), we can turn the thermostat up (COE). We are changing the environment to make the room warmer and reducing both CFE and CFI. If the room has no heat or we do not want the room warmer, we can dress warmer (COE). We can hop around and swing our arms or stomp our feet and hands (COE). More can be accomplished if we find some activity, such as cleaning house or a daily exercise to generate energy to combat the cold (COE).

Controls FI and OI evolve primarily from internal events. As with external forces, sometimes we can control internal impulses; other times we either can not or choose not to do so. We can respond to hunger pangs (CFI) by eating, which makes them go away. We can learn to ignore them (COI), up to a point. We can respond to anger by lashing out and hitting someone or something causing ourselves greater pain and problems. We can channel that energy into finding options for solving the problems that are causing the anger. For example, we can change our relationship with the person with whom we are angry or change our behavior to solve the problem. Remember to look at all the options, we have those choices!

These examples show that we can achieve Self-Direction in several ways. Sometimes we can reduce the amount of control FI or FE; other times we must increase control OI or OE. The absolute amount of control is not as important as the relationship of each source of control to each other source, and the balance that can be created between them.

Remember the LIFE PRESERVER in Chapter 3! Also important to remember is the fact that we are dealing with our experience. Remember that what we experience is not always what really occurs. We can change the balance of control with the environment or internal impulses without changing the reality of them. We remember a plane flight to Europe that was crowded and uncomfortable but calm. It was a steady flight without weather problems. We were amazed to hear another passenger complain about how rough the flight had been. She claimed that the plane had been tossed around with such force that she was bruised black and blue for days afterward! We joked that she must of ridden in the luggage compartment. The only bruises we incurred were from riding the roller coaster at Tivoli.

Imagine a new employee joins the office staff whom you believe to be a threat to your progress. As long as you believe the person is a threat, the four sources of control shift in magnitude so that you feel increased control CFE (the employee), fear, and helplessness (our response CFI). Then a colleague whom you trust assures you that the new person is harmless. Consequently, your control CFE drops and your previous control COE is restored to its original magnitude. Note the new employee did not change at all, only your perception changed, based on trust in a colleague.

Now, imagine that the new employee really is a threat. To reduce that threat CFE, you can exert control COE. You can try to make the new employee your ally and form a friendly, collaborative relationship so he does not go after your job. You can be more effective at your job so you are less vulnerable. You can try to find a way to get him fired. Such action, while it may restore your balance of control temporarily, may prove to be self-destructive in the end.

These examples show that a change in the balance of control OE and FE can occur because of the decrease of one, the increase of the other, or changes in both. The same is true for control FI and OI.

Are You Always In Control?

The examples above show that control OE must dominate over control FE in most situations most of the time. However, there are exceptions. In the give and take of marital relationships, some child-parent relationships, and other situations requiring collaboration, each partner allows the other greater COE in certain well-defined situations. Traditionally, husbands control family finances and decisions such as where the family will live based upon his job. Wives commonly direct the care and education of the children. Changing marital and family relationships and roles provide other options. Those who choose not to follow traditional rules must make their own. They must agree on which partner will exert control in which situations. The rule of the marriage will give most of the responsibility for the house and children to the wife. In return, she stays some distance from her husband's work and employment decisions.

Marriages and similar collaborative relationships in which neither partner exerts control in any single situation usually have dramatic problems of their own. Not exerting or experiencing control is rarely a workable option. It is a laissez-faire (doing what you want) situation, which is frequently mistaken for being democratic. If we have been out for a day's drive but neither of us can decide where to stop for dinner, we are likely to eat at a place that is unsatisfactory for both. Many a potential romance has withered because each partner has been reluctant to commit himself or herself to an activity that they might enjoy for fear of being insensitive to the other's desires. Parents often lose control of their child in child-rearing practices because they fear that if they discipline the child they will lose the love of their child. Sometimes they are afraid of showing their own anger (CFI). Very often, this occurs because of the lack of structure and the traditions that used to guide us as a child. Sometimes with new families in different times, we build our own traditions.

Just as we must exert some control over the environment, we must also feel control OI over control FI in most situations. If we did not, our impulses would blow us along through life. People can not live together in societies without developing enough control OI to keep from hurting each other. There are times when we purposefully decrease control OI so that we deliberately experience the environment and ourselves in different ways. Examples include giving up to an artistic or sexual experience, drinking alcohol, and taking drugs. Obviously, some kinds of loss of control are more socially acceptable than others. Shifting ones CFI's from alcohol or drugs to religion or zealous volunteer work may be socially more acceptable but the relationship of COI to CFI may remain the same, only the situation or motivation has changed.

SELF-CONTROL VERSUS ENVIRONMENTAL CONTROL

Self-control (COI), or lack of it, is learned early, usually in response to parental discipline, and is incorporated as an influence from the environment. For instance, the parent tells a child he or she must not do something (CFE), such as stand up on chairs to reach the goodies in the kitchen cabinets. The next time the same incident comes up, the child tells him- or herself that he or she cannot do something (COI). This is the process of development and maturity – just as it was in toilet training.

The relationship between parental discipline (CFE) and the development of self-control demonstrates that what happens in the environment can affect what happens inside us. A universal example is toilet training. We have long recognized that parental style in toilet training effects the child's development of control. Other examples include delaying sexual activity until after marriage or not drinking too much, both COI functions. Today we teach that moderate drinking is okay, but not drinking and driving. In most cases, control FE remains strong until control OI takes over with maturity. Usually, control FE is high initially while control OI is low when the individual is young, and then as control OI develops, controls FE decreases. This relationship continues throughout life. Obviously, the nature of CFEs in early childhood plays a significant role in the development of COIs. The parents who impose no environmental restraints (CFE) on their children raise children without the proper development of COI. Frequently the child has no ability to recognize appropriate CFE's, which of course leads to a great deal of trouble.

Recent decades have put less emphasis on controlling one's behavior than did earlier decades. The 1960s' slogan "do your own thing" expresses this social change. To demonstrate this trend, we repeated a study first conducted 20 years earlier. We wanted to find out whether today's college freshmen showed the same Experienced Control profile as freshmen had two decades earlier. We sampled a group at a large midwestern university that we had studied earlier. Only one component had changed over these 20 years. CFI had increased significantly, suggesting that we have become a more impulse-driven society. After all, we "only go around once," so why not "seize the day"? Such slogans have become more common in recent years.

We re-tested a group of people after eight years to see how they changed. Our most significant finding was that the women were less inclined to control their impulses (COI) than they had eight years earlier. Clearly, much has changed in the last few decades that directly affect our impulses and our desire to control them. We have more relaxed attitudes about sex and social behaviors. Our greater awareness of bizarre and indiscriminate acts of crime and violence is resulting in greater laws, prisons, and screening procedures (CFEs), but less growth of programs for developing more responsible COIs (self-discipline).

Effect of Internal Forces on the Environment

How do we make people more aware of the CFIs and the CFEs so they can develop greater and more appropriate COIs and COEs? Just as external forces build our responses to internal influences, what happens inside us can change the environment. If we feel anger toward another person (CFI) and have the control OE of a Mafia don, we could alter the environment by ordering an enemy's death. If we feel awe at a beautiful sunset and have the control OE of an artist, we can paint our vision for others to enjoy for years to come.

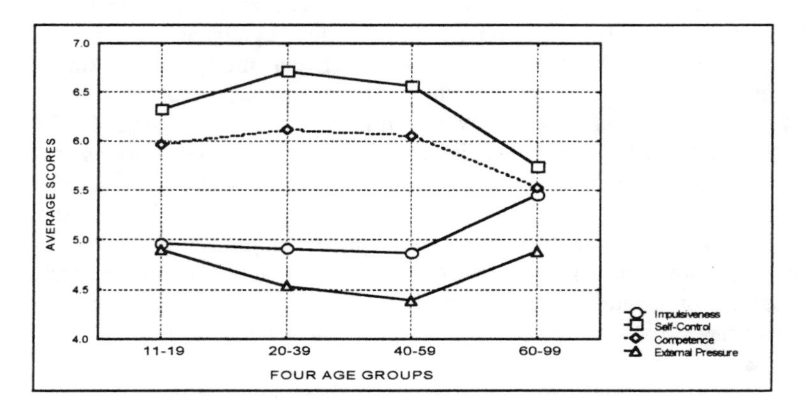

FIGURE 11. CONTROL COMPONENTS BY AGE.

The four kinds of control by age groups in Figure 11, using 3608 nonpsychiatric subjects, are significantly different [$F(9,10815)=23.55$; $p<.0001$]. The two "over" components (COI, COE) show the highest scores and the two "from" components (CFI, CFE) show the lowest. The components interact significantly with the age groups, showing the most dramatic change in the oldest age group (60 to 99). For example, the CFI and CFE components raise sharply for this group denoting the experience of increased internal and external pressures the older we get.

At the same age period, COI and COE show a sudden drop, recognizing that Self-Direction is limited and NonSelf-Direction is increased as we age. These are ideal conditions for feeling a loss of control, but unable to do anything about it. Dr. Karl Menninger was asked on his 85th birthday what it was like. He replied, "I feel like a young man who has something wrong with him." Perhaps the loss of Self-Direction takes the biggest toll we can conceive. The psychological state leaves us feeling powerless with little or no control, and older people do not feel there is a way to remedy the situation. In fact, the significant loss of coping for the elderly is greater than with psychiatric outpatients and, in some cases, reaches the level of suicide.[21]

Using impulses from within and appropriate, well-developed methods for achieving control over the environment can result in an enormous amount of focused power. Such power can be used to destructive or constructive ends. Both Adolph Hitler and Winston Churchill could match their expressions CFI with highly developed political skills to achieve the control they sought over their worlds. Such power can work within marriages and families with just as much force.

CREATIVITY AND CONTROL

"Creativity" is a combination of high CFI and COE which results in forms of expression. While its reverse, high control CFE and COI can weaken us into nearly total inhibition and restraint. A study of emotionally disturbed and normal pre-adolescents (eight-, ten-, and twelve-year-old males) illustrated this point using a creative task. We asked all three groups of children what they would do if caught in a bubble and floated into space. Emotionally disturbed children, who were psychiatric day patients, said they would smother and die. Nonpsychiatric children said they would fly around, explore space, and visit the stars. When they got tired, they said they would fly home and pop their bubbles. These children were measured using pictorial stimuli of Control to Freedom from Control. The emotionally disturbed kids experienced significantly more control from others than normal kids. The experienced control is an obvious indicator of emotional problems and it starts very young.

We respond in various ways to situations that call on creativity. Imagine that you are a student assigned to write a theme. Although you try to tackle the assignment, you are constantly thinking that your teacher will dislike what you have written and give you a bad grade (control FE). These thoughts inhibit you so much that you can barely function, let alone write with any kind of creative impact (CFI plus COE). To unleash creativity and complete your assignment successfully, you need to reduce your fears CFI or increase your control COE. You can accomplish this by employing tactics such as re-reading earlier papers that the teacher liked, or choosing a topic you know the teacher cannot resist.

More productively, we can try to understand what experience has caused us to believe that the teacher will dislike our work. Understand what is driving these negative thoughts. If that is not possible, (there are times when such probing requires professional guidance), put all your energy into seeing how creative you can be. The teacher may not like the product but you should certainly get some responses that will help sort out the dilemma for the next assignment. Of course, you can always drop the class, escaping to a 'safe' environment in which you no longer feel threatened. That perception of safety will not last because when unresolved fear determines your behavior, a new fear will likely take the place of the old one in the new environment.

COMFORT AND CONTROL

While being in control is usually preferable, it is not always comfortable. It is sometimes easier to follow orders, whether in the army, at work, or in a family, than to assert our opinion. Sometimes it is hard assuming responsibility when in charge or for accepting blame if something goes wrong. Similarly, controlling internal impulses rather than giving in to them may give rise to all sorts of conflict and tension. If you have tried to stop smoking, or if you are responding as a co-dependent in a relationship, you already know this.

You do not have to be smarter than other people to learn control COI and COE; you simply have to work constantly at building an even greater repertoire of problem solving skills. You also must learn to expect to feel in control. *People who expect to be in charge of their lives achieve more than those who do not, and those who do not expect to be in charge, even though they are extremely bright or talented, do not achieve what they could.*

ACHIEVEMENT AND CONTROL

Control has a positive side. It has a lot to do with achievement. If you experience yourself as an insignificant person, you will act as if you are insignificant. For example, you may not write a letter to an elected official "because they don't read my letters anyway." You may not compete in school or at work with your friend "because she's always beaten you in the past." You may not start the business you have always wanted "because nobody knows what the economy is going to do." Yet, people do write letters, compete, and start new businesses. The difference between those who do and those who do not is the experience of personal control leading to Self-Direction. Although two people's circumstances are essentially the same, one may be more willing than the other to take the gamble. The person who is encouraged by experienced control is likely to succeed in a new venture, and that success builds greater experienced control, ever enlarging their repertoire of problem solving and coping skills. The experience of control reinforces itself! The problem we face is knowing the boundaries of appropriateness.

Sidney was an agoraphobic (fear of public places; CFE) with panic attacks (CFI) he had experienced for 15 years. Individual psychotherapy taught him to expand his comfort zone, his hiding place. Each step away from his home led to greater and greater rewards as he overcame the CFE's through relaxation techniques, which, in turn, reduced the occurrence of panic attacks (CFI). These accomplishments were self-rewarding and reinforced his efforts to push harder to venture into new areas that he first saw as threatening. The former CFEs no longer existed. New COEs emerged and he enjoyed the expansiveness of his life that had been restricted to a few blocks from his job and home. Today he is a CEO of a bank and can handle bank mergers and other matters with no fear of venturing into the unknown. He even bought a new house in a new neighborhood far from where he used to live. He enjoys throwing social parties, which to him was the ultimate in overcoming control FE.

The first step in solving control problems is identifying specifically the nature of the problem, which is discussed in detail in Chapter 5.

---

[21] Tiffany, D.W. and Tiffany, P.G. 1996. Control across the life span: A model for understanding self-direction. *Journal of Adult Development*, 3, 2, 93-108.

Chapter 5: Control Problems

THE KEYS TO CONTROL

The invitation to your spouse's annual office party just arrived, and when you open it, you realize you do not want to go. You have too much work to do. You are busy every other night that week, and you want to spend one quiet evening at home. Besides, you never seem to know what to say to those people. They always talk shop, and you feel invisible. Anyway, your spouse has been thinking about changing jobs, so why put up with the aggravation?

You have listed four reasons for staying at home, but none is as compelling as it seems. Let us examine each one. You are not going to work that night even if you do not go to the party. You have learned that a full day of work is enough, and putting in more hours rarely produces results. Sure, a night at home would be relaxing, but nothing is going on the following weekend, and you will have plenty of time to unwind. Your spouse's colleagues talk shop with each other, but their spouses do not, and with a little effort, you might find some new friends among them. Your spouse is talking about changing jobs. That is because he was passed over for a promotion! You think your spouse is embarrassed. You were certainly embarrassed for him. That is the real reason why you do not want to go to the party. You know it the minute you think over the situation.

Experienced Control Theory calls the critical response to the invitation the "focal determinant." It gives you a key to resolving the situation. The other aspects, pressure to ignore work, sacrifice relaxation, and subjecting yourself to boredom, are "contextual[22] determinants," and focusing on them obscures the source of our discomfort. Claiming that you have too much to do and that you want to spend a quiet evening at home, or that you have nothing in common with your spouse's colleagues may result in interesting discussions.

However, they do not solve the problem at hand. Discussing your spouse's embarrassment, and especially yours for him, gets to the significant issue.

Your discussion with him might produce some surprises. You might find that your spouse is not at all embarrassed by not receiving the promotion. The colleague who was promoted was far more experienced than he and, by everyone's measure, deserved the job. Your spouse felt flattered to even be considered for the position and thinks he has a good chance next time. Given all of this, attending the party and showing everyone that you are both team players with no hard feelings could further your spouse's career.

On the other hand, you may find your suspicions confirmed. Your spouse may well be embarrassed and hate the thought of facing the group. In that case, you can agree to stay home, or go, as your spouse desires. Your spouse will see you as willing to stand by him through good and bad. Whatever the outcome, you have strengthened a bond with your spouse, and together you are exerting control over the environmental sea in which your marriage floats.

DETERMINANTS OF CONTROL FROM ALL DIRECTIONS

In the simple example above, both the focal and contextual determinants were responses (COE) to control from the environment (CFE). In other cases, other sources of control might be at work. We might want to start our own business, an ambitious drive (CFI plus COE). We may also believe that the economy is too uncertain (CFE), competition is too stiff (CFE) and we might not have what it takes to survive (CFI), such as "fire in the belly" for achieving our goals.

Resolving your conflict quickly and efficiently requires that you identify which of competing stimuli is the focal or most significant determinant. This is not always easy. Sometimes it takes a lot of sorting out of different feelings and experiences, even discussions with others. Then, you must create a strategy for addressing the most important determinant. If we are confident we can succeed, we frequently do. We can hedge against an uncertain economy by diversifying our investments. We can find investments that are considered the most "recession proof." We can carve a niche in which we can survive. If we doubt our own abilities, we can work to strengthen them or find a partner with strengths where we are weak. We can find a way to surmount any difficulty, but to do that swiftly and effectively starts when we recognize what is bothering us, i.e., where we feel an absence of control in terms of the focal versus contextual factors.

FOCAL AND CONTEXTUAL DETERMINANTS

If a witness to a crime sees the perpetrator brandishing some kind of weapon, the witness later remembers less about the perpetrator than the weapon. Several studies have supported the existence of the 'weapon focus' to the blurring of the context. This happens to us in many situations in which we find ourselves. Some part of the situation may be recalled even better than the situation. On the other hand, some focal determinant is recalled, but the situation is not remembered.

Understanding the characteristics of focal and contextual determinants helps to sort situational qualities quickly. First, either may be specific or general, but the more general the determinant, the greater the likelihood that we have not identified it precisely. Consider a response to a general determinant: "I just do not like those people." Completing the sentence with "because..." helps to get at the specific determinant. "I just do not like those people because they are rude," or "they make me feel inferior," or "They always want to go to expensive, stuffy restaurants." The more complete statement turns a vague sense of discomfort into details with which we can work – on which we can *focus*.

You know the feeling of being bothered by something, but not knowing what or why. Sometimes, conflicting determinants cause that feeling. Imagine that you are stopping to pick up a friend to go to a movie. You arrive at his house a little late and are worried about getting to the theater on time. Your friend is sitting in front of the television, eyes glued to the set, watching wrestling. "I think this violence is terrible," he says without looking at you. You feel a general sense of anger and respond angrily to your friend. You ask yourself "Why the anger?" Is it your concern about getting to the movie? Is it the contradictory messages your friend is sending? Is your response to his message appropriate? Identifying specific determinants, focal (your getting to the movie on time) and contextual (your friend and the TV), helps you understand which determinant is focal and which is contextual so you can respond appropriately.

CONTEXT: FOREGROUND VERSUS BACKGROUND

Sometimes what was a focal determinant quickly fades to become part of the context, if a new focal determinant arises. Imagine dating someone you find very attractive and you are spending an evening at your date's home. Your date is the focal determinant. Candlelight, soft music, and comfortable surroundings form the context. Suddenly the front door bangs open and in walks another of your date's suitors, enraged at the intimate scene. Instantly, the suitor becomes your focal determinant and your date part of the context. Your mood has shifted from seduction to self-defense. The ways in which we want to maintain control over our environment change just as fast. In such situations, our focus shifts and we perceive something else. Focal determinants that contrast sharply with contextual determinants are easier to identify than when the contrast is less sharp. Our date's angry suitor is hard to miss in the otherwise romantic setting. Conversely, the more similar the elements of a situation, the greater our tendency to perceive them as a unit and the more easily we lose the individuality of the elements.

Imagine that you are watching your child play ball across the street with neighbor children. Your child is the focal determinant. Suddenly he hits the ball through the neighbor's window. Just as suddenly, all the children become the focal determinant. They were all playing ball, and seeing them as a unit saves us from having to focus on our child as having made the mistake alone. This is using the context to our advantage.

THE ULTIMATE FOCUS

So far, we have talked about focal determinants as if they were all that really mattered. Eliminating or ignoring contextual determinants some times leads to an efficient form of solving control problems. That approach is heavy concentration or focus. Imagine that you are playing a round of golf. If you worry that rain will cut the game short or that taking a day off will put you behind at work, you will be unable to concentrate on the shot at hand. That shot is the focal determinant but your thoughts are on a contextual stimulus. Great athletes and performers learn to eliminate contextual distractions and concentrate on a single focal determinant – the task or play, such as making the goal.

Many successful people have been able to achieve because of their ability to focus on a single goal without the interference of irrelevant context. This is true in every occupation. Great public and private accomplishments such as those from teachers, parents, skilled artists or local delivery persons result from focus. They learn to focus on what is important and put aside the rest. Imagine the basketball player at the free-throw line with the many distractions set up by the opposing supporters behind the basket backboard. The sharper the contrast between the focal and contextual stimuli, the better he or she will do.

Another common experience of context is when we hear someone 'take something out of context' to argue their point. This happens frequently in court when trial lawyers quote the witness 'our of context' to support their argument. Many times the context, when added, completely changes the meaning of the focal argument.

Let us also note that contextual determinants can be very important and should not always be ignored in our perceptions, whether our perception is to make a basket or formulate a new foreign policy. Contextual determinants are important to understand, for they effect our response to, and options for dealing with, the focal determinant. For a simple example, let us investigate the effects of a frame (contextual) for a picture (focal). Imagine that a person you barely know lectures you sternly on the morality of your behavior. Imagine further that this lecture occurs in the church you have faithfully attended for years. Now, change the background image and imagine that this lecture takes place on the sidelines of the high school football game. Same lecture, but the dramatically different context creates dramatically different interactions between the focal stimulus and the context in your perception of the meaning of the lecture, and particularly, your response.

Another example of the importance of context is the romantic vacation spot. There you are with the same beloved partner, and you are your same old self, but the romantic-get-away brings about quite a change. Rather than carrying your problems and stress with you, you blend into the environment and choose to allow the "love boat" phenomenon to take over (CFI). This is a case where the frame makes the picture. This frame effect is what Hollywood tries to capture with every movie.

Some times the picture makes the frame; and, some times, they do equal justice to each other, whether it is bad or good. When carried to the extreme, such as sensory depravation, there is essentially no context, which can be frightening, and the focal stimulus is the thoughts we have. When we remove the loud music from some teenagers and they are left with only their thoughts; we sometimes find interesting effects – as we would in a sensory depravation experiment!

Contextual determinants warrant attention of their own. Consider contextual determinants that disappear, or are ignored, when the focal determinant fades. For example, headaches produce pain, strong CFI focal determinants. The headache is surrounded by many contextual determinants including worries about their causes. Does the headache signal a more serious illness? Tension? Emotional conflict? All of these worries are contextual determinants. If any one of the worries requires major changes, they will likely not be pursued. The possible problems could require medical diagnosis and treatment, living differently to reduce tension, or dealing with emotional problems. Changes we would prefer to avoid. Therefore, when the headache stops, we ignore the contextual determinants that accompanied it, although they may be signals that need our attention. It has always been fascinating in psychotherapy to learn when patients recover from their illness they also report that world events seem to have improved at the same time! Psychotherapists like to joke that they not only treat the patient, but they also treat the world simultaneously. Maybe it is true!

The more conscious you are of the contexts in which focal determinants occur, the better you will be in solving control problems. Imagine that you have an appointment at 4:30 in the afternoon that will take nearly an hour, and you have to pick up your child from day care before 5:30 p.m. You worry that you will not make it to day care before 5:30 p.m. You could spend the afternoon stewing around in the general control FE, or you can separate the focal determinant from the context in the situation to increase your control. If your focal determinant is pressure CFE to pick up your child on time, you can cancel or change the time of your business appointment. You can ask your spouse to pick up your child on the way home from work. If none of these choices is viable, you can call the person with whom you are to meet and request that the meeting start and end at times convenient for you to pick up your child on time. Alternatively, when you go to your meeting, simply tell them you have to leave earlier than planned. Lastly, you can call the day care provider to explain your tight schedule and request that someone stay a few minutes if you are late. If these ideas are not possible, you will have to reschedule.

Although such situations are seemingly simple, even trivial, every day is a series of one situation after the next where focal and contextual reversals exist that do not necessarily work together. Several of them can build stress in minutes. The important message is that there are many ways of reducing the pressures. However, we often do not think through and isolate the choices available. They tend to get all clumped together. Exercising control in situations not only prevents stress, it also boosts the skill and self-esteem needed to tackle the bigger control problems life presents. We have all admired the individual that is able to maintain the tight schedule and never seems ruffled. Such behavior is by design and lots of practice.

Other interesting characteristics about focus and context (frame) is the emphasis we put on one or the other. For example, we can be almost entirely focused on something and not be aware of the context. Conversely, we can be almost entirely contextual-oriented and not be focused on anything specific. In the former case, an individual can be focused on a task until it is complete and then shift to another task without being aware of the context, which may be one's family. Being overly task-oriented frequently omits the emotional environment, which is the context, and the family feels they are not a part of the individual's life. The other extreme is a preoccupation with the context without focusing on anything. This individual is overly sensitive to everyone and everything around them to the exclusion of focusing on anything in particular. Such individuals rarely achieve very much, but they are very much in touch with those around them. The former case of being task-oriented generally nets a big gain in achievement for the individual, but it leaves them emotionally isolated and disconnected with those around them. Obviously, a balance between the focus and context, depending on the situation, is best while using each in an appropriate way over the course of time.

CHANGING FOCUS

After analyzing determinants closely, you can change determinants, moving them from context to focus and back. You may think, "Wait a minute, what's so critical about the 4:30 appointment? Even one you have waited months for, is easier rescheduled than worried about."

Friends coming for dinner? You can focus on your desire to impress them with your fabulous cooking and knock yourself out preparing a seven-course meal. You know you will be distracted and not enjoy their company. You know too, that you will be totally exhausted when they leave. You could ask them to help in the kitchen; a technique for built-in companionship and entertainment that also gets the job done and reduces stress. On the other hand, you can focus on enjoying their company by taking them out to eat.

FRACTIONATING

Another concept in Experienced Control Theory is called "fractionating." Our studies have shown that when control from the environment (CFE) increases, our responses from within (CFI) increase as well, up to a point. These may be emotional or physiological, such as anger or an upset stomach. This surge of response from within is our attempt to fend off overpowering control FE.

Any one who has felt such responses knows that they are not pleasant, and rarely productive. Getting angry at your boss for giving you a distasteful assignment, or even talking calmly about your distaste, may not be realistic choices for you. The context may tell you that your boss will fire you the instant you object to an order and it may also remind you that you cannot afford to be fired. If you are to live comfortably with the assignment, your only option is to divide the perceived control FE so that only its positive aspects are your focal determinant. A brief case may help understand the term fractionation as it applies to every day living.

It is rare that emotionally disturbed individuals are disturbed equally in all situations. Before entering individual outpatient psychotherapy, Jean would fractionate her environment into separate 'do-able' activities, such as child and house care. We all have our "safe havens" or our "third place."[23] Jean maintained her emotional stability by engaging in activities in her safe havens (reduced CFEs), when interacting with others outside the home was more than she could handle. However, as the children begin leaving home, Jean was pushed more and more into group activities (CFE) with dire consequences. Her marital problems escalated, which led to her entering treatment. She obtained extremely low coping scores in all situations using the Tiffany Control Scales[24]. She was clinically depressed to the point of being suicidal (COI = 2.75 and COE = 2.88; CFI = 6.75 and CFE = 6.75; Coping = -7.87) in the standard situations of "Work," "School," "Opposite Sex," "Same Sex," "Community," "Home," "Other People," and "Self-in-General." These scores showed her highly NonSelf-Directed. Consequently, Jean was asked to fractionate her environment to come up with situations in which she was best able to cope. She listed art, gardening, housekeeping, cooking, and raising her two children. When the Tiffany Control Scales was customized with these five new situations, Jean's results showed that she was able to have reasonable control over a part of her life that did not indicate suicidal thoughts. In fact, she was Self-Directed in these areas. What does this mean? With greater treatment emphasis on her fractionated interests, Jean was better able to hang on until treatment progressed far enough that she could handle ordinary every-day situations that were stressful to her. Today, Jean is happy, outgoing, and does not feel any situation is beyond her ability – and she is right! Her Tiffany Control Scales scores improved significantly in response to treatment (COI = 5.43 and COE = 6.1; CFI = 5.83 and CFE = 4.95; Coping = .75). She is significantly more Self-Directed in all areas.

COMMON USE OF FRACTIONATION

Several years ago when repeated airplane hijackings first provoked tightened airport security, many travelers objected to what they perceived as an invasion of their privacy. They felt high control FE and responded with outrage and indignation (CFI). Later, they came to perceive the situation differently, and their outcries died down. First, because everyone was being searched, no one felt individually embarrassed, and over time, the searches became routine before boarding. Second, travelers realized that tightened security contributed to, rather than reduced, their sense of control OE.

Air travelers realized that if their flights were hijacked, they would never reach their destinations on schedule, and maybe never at all. What they first perceived as negative they now saw as having positive and negative aspects. Now the positive outweighed the negative. Third, while focusing on the positive aspect, they perceived the searches as broader contextual determinants that protected their safety. The result? Instead of perceiving control from the environment as a threat to privacy, at worst and an imposition at best, they began to fractionate the perception and see it as an advantage. They confirmed, "Now our families do not have to worry about where we will end up every time we board a plane and neither do we."

Such processes go on among parents all the time. Parents of adolescents often feel that they must exert absolute control over their children when their behavior stumbles occasionally. Parents may perceive their teenager's behavior as a pressure CFE and are unable to assign a focal cause to specific behaviors, which frequently leads to treating the problem as contextual, thus alienating the child. Example: a 13-year-old was found to have beer on his breath and the parents assumed he has been coming home this way for months. Consequently, he had to have his breath tested every time he came home and had to be home earlier than before. Later it was found he had simply tried a beer that one night and decided he disliked it.

In contrast to addressing the child about such matters are parents who were inhibited from directing appropriate concerns toward the child and turn their feelings inward. We then hear evidence of them blaming themselves: "Where did we go wrong?" "Why did we fail?"

Most parents deal with adolescents' unpredictable behavior by separating the good from the bad and assigning the bad a broader context – right or wrong. "They're pretty good students, and all this moping around is just a stage they're going through" is frequently heard. This focuses on the kids' strengths, assigns a broad context of internal pressure, and fractionates their weaknesses from being good students. "This fascination with fast cars comes from the gang they run around with," assigns a context of external pressure as well as fractionates the CFE to acknowledge that 'fast cars' is not something they came up with on their own.

The blame for violent behavior that many people put on weapons, media, movies, gangs, etc. is a form of fractionating. It allows us to continue to believe that people, particularly children, are not "bad." Rather, the circumstances of their lives are thought to lead them astray.

It is as though human nature is by default irresponsible and NonSelf-Directed. It is amazing the number of individuals who came from a bad background that are responsible and are successful as Self-Directed persons! Fractionating in this matter can be carried to extremes, such as with law suits that want to sue corporations (tobacco, guns, liquor, etc.) or professionals (not taking your pills). Where will fractionating the responsibility end; with alcohol producers, farmers because of producing foods that make us overweight, firework manufactures because we did not read the warning? When is the responsibility ours? How can we become Self-Directed in such a climate of making everybody else responsible?

The Power of Choice

Of course, we have all known parents who fractionate some behaviors, but are only kidding themselves; their kids, in fact, are criminals. We know of severely battered spouses, who explain, "I'm sure he loves me. He just doesn't know how to show it." "I was just following orders" is an effort to fractionate oneself from some of the most heinous crimes of the twentieth century. When does our fractionation of determinants change from healthy to foolish to downright destructive and violent? How many times have we heard that drinking alcohol was the cause of his behavior that led to the death of someone?

Many times, we allow determinants to change without conscious awareness of what we are letting happen to us. Social scientists and governments frequently use the process of teaching people to make choices by using just noticeable differences. We learned to accept the change in the price of bread from 10 cents in 1945 to more than a dollar in 1999 because we understand the inflationary process created by the increased quality of life. As citizens, we accept more and more regulation and government control – to a point. Even while we rile against such encroachments, we find ourselves on an unending slide toward more regulation because we accepted it in small increments over many years. Had we suddenly been taken over by a foreign government, we would bear arms to fight the encroachment. Instead, we begrudgingly except slow change in just noticeable degrees that, some would argue, amount to the same result of a government takeover. When we realize what has happened, we hear cries of "Too much government and it needs to be downsized."

VALIDITY GENERALIZATION

In a study we recently published regarding applied issues in psychological testing,[25] we questioned whether validity generalization measures of personality vary across samples in different situations. Traditionally, we generalize a concept across situations and infer that the concept will continue to show similar test characteristics, even when situations change. Kurt Lewin[26] conceived of the individual's life space, which opened the way to exploring these situation-behavior relationships. Later, Walter Mischel[27] and others examined the situation-behavior association showing predictive accuracy between behaviors and contexts. These investigators critically reproached the assumed validity generalization of assessment instruments that ignore contextual variance. The hypothesis of our study confirmed that using individual scales fails to focus on the contextual effects on the concept, and consequently fails to have practical application for focused evaluation in many clinical and employment settings. Earlier, we described the Experienced Control Model, and how a measurement of *contextual variance*, in personality dimensions, allows situation specificity. Later, we will extend the application for more focused treatment and job fit in employment settings.

There are no simple answers – every situation is different. What remains constant is that in every situation, we are making choices, whether we see them as choices or not. Many times these choices are productive and strengthen us. Our values help us select the best one. Larry, for instance, chose not to shoot the bear in part because he did not believe in the unnecessary killing of animals. The process of analyzing and evaluating the options we face, creating new ones when we can, and enacting the most effective choice helps us gain control. It also equips us with the vision to see our choices for what they are and to make them consistent with the values we hold dear. Chapter 6 goes into more detail about broader systems that may exert control over us. It provides some techniques for reducing the control over us in these systems.

---

[22] Tiffany, D.W. and Tiffany, P.G. 1996. Contextual effects on adolescent disorders relevant to coping, *Psychological Reports*, 78, 593-594.

[23] "Home" and "Work" are the first and second place in our lives. The third place is what we like to do for ourselves. Sometimes, it can be referred to as a hobby.

[24] The Tiffany Control Scales allows screening from a sixth grade reading level to age 99. It assesses variables such as 'coping' and 'assertive' level, as well as 'self' versus 'other' orientation for any situation, while also examining four types of control problems. Sixteen personality variables are measured and are broken out by any situation the examiner is interested in screening.

[25] Tiffany, D.W. and Tiffany, P.G. 1999. Overgeneralization of validity generalization in personality inventories: Applied issues in testing, *Psychological Reports*, 84, 593-609.

[26] Lewin, K. 1943. Defining the Field at a Given Time. *Psychological Review*, 50, 292-310.

[27] Mischel, W. 1977. The interaction of person and situation. In D. Magnusson and N. S. Endler. eds. *Personality at the crossroads: Current issues in interactional psychology*. Hillsdale, N. J: Erlbaum.

Chapter 6: Hospitals or Asylums

SEPARATE WORLDS

In 1961, Erving Goffman[28] studied prisons, hospitals, military reservations, naval vessels, boarding schools, monasteries, and nursing homes. His work, Asylums, describes the "total" institution as, "A place of residence and work where a large number of like-situated individuals, cut off from the wider society for an appreciable period of time, together lead an enclosed, formally administered...life." Goffman's findings aptly describe medical hospitals as well as prisons, which have dramatic implications for the institutional treatment of illness. His thesis is that the situation, that is the inmate's reactions and adjustments to the institution, are the determiners of the individual's health and behavior even more than the treatment, in many cases.

Goffman made four points that pertain to the application of the Experienced Control Model to hospitalization. First, in the total institution, the staff and inmates live in two separate worlds. Second, on entering the total institution, the inmates are depersonalized by becoming a number with no privacy. Third, the inmates have less control over their environment in the total institution than "on the outside." Finally, because of depersonalization and loss of control, the inmates of the total institution feel much anxiety and stress.

Total institutional situations do not permit healing and growth. Let us look at the potentially destructive conditions that develop under these circumstances. Then we will look at ways we might change those circumstances.

As Goffman observed about total institutions, hospital staff and patients live in two separate worlds. When the patient enters the hospital, he or she takes on the role of "sick person," part of an implicit contract between the patient and society. Under this contract, the patient has the right to be dependent, the right to expect help from strangers, the right to believe he or she should and can be helped, and the right to be excused from normal obligations. The patient is not expected to be able to help him or herself. Interactions among the patient and hospital staff are shaped by this contract even before the patient begins treatment. If either party to the contract fails to live up to its terms, the contract determines the behavior of both parties. Furthermore, the contract separates patients from hospital staff, who act as agents of society. Incidentally, part of the contract is that you are to wear that flimsy, paper (sometimes cloth) gown that ties in the back.

These views are supported by a comprehensive analysis of the dual social order in hospitals in Sickness and Society by R. S. Duff and A. B. Hollingshead[29] and continues to be supported to this day.

DEPERSONALIZATION

From the moment patients enter a medical hospital they are depersonalized so that the staff can more readily manage them. The sick adult has now made a tacit agreement with the hospital that he or she will proffer his or her body in exchange for intervention in the disease process. The institution is in possession of the patient's body, which encourages (requires) the patient to be dependent on the staff. It is all in the guise of helping the patient. Since the patients believe that he/she needs that help, the contract seems reasonable – at first.

Some hospital advocates argue that dependency is necessary for the patients' own good. Other writers suggest that regression to a pre-adult state during hospitalization is not so much encouraged by the staff as by the patient as a defense mechanism. It would seem that even the admission process begins the patient's dependency. Regardless of his or her age, severity of illness, and any number of other variables, the patient is tagged with a wristband. The message is that the patient cannot be trusted even to remember his or her own name, regardless of the diagnosis. The patient (inmate) is put into bed like an infant, in that flimsy, embarrassing gown. You feel like a child put in a corner of the room for punishment. The patient is expected to submit passively to the scrutiny of strangers. No one pays attention to what the patient wants or says. Every question brings the same answer, "Talk to your doctor," who of course is never available. The patient is told when to sleep, when to eat, when to drink, when to talk, when to defecate, and when to urinate and when to take another test, even if their meal is waiting. What was previously an independently functioning adult is now a regressed, passive and frequently angry patient being described as "good" if he or she remains dependent and "bad" if independence flares up!

Two amusing accounts of this process – amusing only if we are not living through them at the time – can be found in Tom Wolfe's The Right Stuff and Norman Cousins' Anatomy of an Illness. Wolfe describes how even our highly valued astronauts were subjected to the most degrading of situations while assessing their physical fitness. Cousins argues convincingly of the need to deal more with the hospital system than with illness itself. Less amusing are his many accounts of technique's hospital staff use to make patients dependent and, thus, more manageable.

The authors recall a close friend who was being admitted to the hospital for testing. Paper work was to be completed in the afternoon with nothing scheduled for the evening. Arrangements previously had been made for her and her grandson to come to our home for dinner. The evening was not pleasant. Our friend was extremely anxious, not about the outcome of the testing, but because she had left the hospital. She felt that once she had checked into the hospital she had no right to her own desires or time. Before she left, a member of the hospital staff had pointed out that her leaving after checking in was "just not done." The lecture had made her frightened, defensive, and anxious. No amount of rational conversation on our part or from her usually influential grandson could decrease her feelings of guilt. She knew she would have done nothing but spend an idle evening sitting in a lonely room, becoming anxious about the coming morning, causing her anxiety that could be harmful. She felt she had done something terrible to the hospital staff and her doctors that she would somehow pay for.

Loss Of Control Over The Environment

Because of physical affliction, the hospital patient obviously has less control over what is happening to him or her than a person who is not ill. Outside a hospital, a person has the right to give information about himself or herself to other people or to withhold it. In the hospital, the patient is expected to tell all, but only in answer to intake questions. If the question is not on the form, the patient's concern about it is of no interest.

Next, the patient is assigned a roommate, whether one is wanted or not. It matters not if the roommate is congenial, only that the arrangements are convenient for the staff. Even hospital designers seem part of the conspiracy, designing hospitals for double rooms that make the cost of a single room even more prohibitive. Not to be outdone by designers is the Joint Commission for the Accreditation of Hospitals. They demand so much in the way of equipment in the hospital and particularly in each room, that very little time or money is left to add the human touch.

In our own homes, even in hotel rooms we rent, we have the right to prevent others from entering. We can arrange the furniture to suit us, control the thermostat for our comfort. Hospitals, which are more costly than hotel rooms, control whether or not someone enters our room. In fact, someone may be coming and going all day and night. The result is that there is no territory to call one's own when a paying "guest" in a hospital.

Clearly, illness itself causes the loss of a certain amount of control over the environment and oneself. Physical limitations affect body image and self-concept. However, compounding the physical loss with the loss of home, loved ones, privacy, and independence sets up a state of powerlessness that is unlike any other experience we have, which does not speed recovery.

Hospital Stress

Writings by psychologists on hospitalization deal with Goffman's fourth observation. Patients of the total institution feel much anxiety and stress. Most writers agree that the major cause of stress during hospitalization is 'not knowing what is going to happen or when it will happen.' In one study, 40 hospitalized children whose mothers were told what to expect, showed fewer indications of physiological stress than a control group of 40 children whose mothers were not so informed. The mothers, who were told what to expect, appeared more calm and confident to their children. The children came to feel this calmness and confidence themselves. The mothers also explained the illness to their children, which helped them to understand the problem and lessen their anxiety.

Can hospital size play a role in how much stress patients feel? A study of 408 medical-surgical patients in hospitals of three different sizes demonstrated that, except for patients with malignancies, patients in large hospitals experienced more stress than patients in small hospitals. Patients with malignancies had a high degree of stress in hospitals of all sizes. Except for the one condition, the size of the hospital has more to do with whether a patient feels anxiety than does the nature of the illness. This finding strongly suggests that circumstances that make us anxious are more related to the aspects of the hospital experience, rather than our sickness.

Duff and Hollingshead interviewed 161 patients as they were admitted to a large hospital. The emotions reported by the patients fell into three categories. Anxiety was reported by 21 percent of the patients. Apprehension was reported by 27 percent and fear was reported by 52 percent. Interestingly, the more serious the diagnosis, the less fear the patient reported about going into the hospital.

Apparently, what these patients were anxious, apprehension, and fearful about was more the hospital than their illness itself, particularly if the illness was more severe. Not a single patient expressed a positive emotional state.

To determine how much loss of control patients feel, an Experienced Control study looked at 35 patients in a medium-sized hospital, including 16 men and 19 women ranging from age 21 to 68, with an average age in the fifties. Each patient replied to the Tiffany Control Scales twice, once when first hospitalized and once after discharge. The scales produced three sets of scores, one for the degree of control patients felt in the hospital, one for the control they felt afterwards, and – as a comparison – one for when they were with "Other People."

Away from the hospital, these patients reported enough control OE to indicate that they did not feel threatened under normal circumstances. However, when they were hospitalized, their experience of control OE dropped dramatically, while control FE increased. For the hospital situation, their ratios of COE to CFE were about half of what they were at home and close to those of psychiatric patients on an inpatient admission ward.

For the "Hospital" situation, the patients' COE/CFE ratios were about 20 percent lower at admittance than at discharge. This finding suggests that they expected their hospitalization to be worse than it actually was. Overall, the scores indicated that the patients felt they could contend with difficulties better after their discharge from the hospital than before they were admitted.

Recovering from an illness would seem to call for experiencing less control FI and FE, not more. How can we do this? As we saw above, hospitalized patients are separated from their families, then cast in roles of dependency by hospital staff. In most hospital situations, it takes a major act of determination for a family member or the patient to find out what is going to happen to them while in the hospital. In contrast, consider the approach at the hospital of Albert Schweitzer at Lambarene. There, the patient's family – including domestic animals – lived with the patient in the hospital compound. It was not hygienic, but it was human, and it worked!

UTOPIAN GENERAL HOSPITAL

INTERPERSONAL ASPECTS OF RECOVERING FROM AN ILLNESS.

A Utopian General Hospital would have several characteristics. Different from the observations by Goffman, staff would be hired for their compassion, concern, and interpersonal skills as well as their medical expertise. Some medical professionals freely admit a preference for working with things rather than people. There is a great deal of valuable "test tube" research work for them. However, we would argue that further research into the interpersonal aspect of health and wellness is needed as well. Let those who find work with people truly satisfying, work with patients and with elements of the system that affects physical and emotional health. The senior author participated in systems research in cooperation with Dr. Larry Appleby in 1961, which evaluated several psychiatric hospitals using a Q-Methodology[30] technique.

The Q-Method allowed the subjects to arrange a group of 'Centeredness statements' on patient care according to 'Most Like Me' to 'Least Like Me.' The statements went from centering primarily on patient care to centering primarily on hospital policy. The results were clear. The authority chain from top to bottom was highly significant and went from emphasizing hospital policy (doctors, Administrators) to patient care (aides and volunteers). In addition, day shifts were more oriented to patient care and night shifts were more oriented to hospital policy. Overall, the validity of the scale was demonstrated by evaluating the data according to wards since some wards are expected to be more hospital-policy oriented. For example, the Admission's ward was more patient-care oriented and the Intensive Care ward was more hospital- policy oriented.

An ideal hospital and medical staff at Utopian General would have a staff of counselors to help patients cope with their illnesses and treatment that have an orientation similar to those that were patient centered in the above study. A public relations or communications expert, that is able to translate the medical goings on to patient and family members, should be available at all times. The effect on family members, relationships, and employment consequences would be anticipated and worked out. Organization-centered (hospital rules are most important) versus patient-centered (patient needs are most important) studies clearly show that some psychiatric hospitals and some wards within these hospitals are more patient-centered than are others. Some treatment groups, such as aides and social workers, are more patient-centered than others, such as physicians and administrators, who tend to be more organization-centered.

At Utopian General, patients would be kept as adult and as human as possible. Their names would be on their doors and in the minds of the staff, not on their wrists (with possible exceptions in situations including brain injury, comas, and in intensive care). They would be told everything about their condition as soon as it was known and efforts would be undertaken to find their doctor when needed. If physicians are so overworked, then get more nurse practitioners to fill in. Whenever possible, family members, even pets, could live with them or at least visit them in rooms set aside for that purpose. Patients would exercise as much control over their lives as possible and not be wheeled everywhere they go if the patient wants the exercise of walking. They would sleep until they are ready to wake up, eat when they are hungry, urinate when their bladders are full, and sleep when they are sleepy without being awakened every two or three hours to take their vital signs. If litigation is the issue here, let the patient sign something entitling them to sleep through the night. Waking up continuously is the same effect they use in torture facilities to keep the individual groggy and helpless! Lastly, for the price they pay, they should be able to choose roommates or private rooms.

Utopian General is not real. However, many of its characteristics cost no more, take no longer, than hospital procedures today. Moreover, in the end, it would bring in more business. The long-term economic savings would be in shorter stays, faster and more effective treatment, less family disorganization, and less work time lost. In general, the cost of illness to society would be greatly lessened.

As patients, we should insist on as many of these innovative characteristics as possible. Undoubtedly, a growing recognition of the value of Utopian General's traits accounts for increased interest in nurse practitioners, hospices, home care, and "walk-in" medical care facilities. Such facilities specialize in women's care, pain management, cardiovascular care, dermatology, otolaryngology, and some provide outpatient surgeries. We know such solutions frequently cost <u>less</u> than traditional hospital stays.

Taking Charge Of Your Surgery Or Hospital Stay

The surgery process can bring up many stressful situations in which control skills will be required for the patient to obtain good care. In addition, being in control may provide increased patient protection during hospitalization. According to Deardorff and Reeves (1998), "The chance of getting an infection during a hospital stay is estimated to be between five and ten percent. Each year, more Americans die from hospital infections than from car accidents and homicides combined. Disturbingly, the Center for Disease Control has found that a great majority of these hospital infections can be prevented," (p.88).[31] In fact, it was reported in the Los Angeles Times in July 1999 that Dr. David Lawrence, Kaiser Permanente's chief executive, told the National Press Club that medical mistakes kill more people each year than tobacco, alcohol, firearms, or automobiles. He stated that medical accidents and mistakes kill 400,000 people a year, ranking behind heart disease and cancer as the leading cause of death.

Make the choice for outpatient surgery when possible and avoid staying in a costly hospital. Increasingly, surgical procedures are conducted in outpatient facilities in a single day or on an overnight basis. However, if you can not avoid a hospital stay, here are some ideas you can put into effect to put you in control even before being admitted.

Learn all you can about your surgery or even why you are in the hospital. Find out about the length of the surgical procedure, hospital stay, and expected recovery. Hospitals frequently have data to show expected success and recovery of different surgical procedures. The Internet has chat forums for just about any surgical procedure or make inquiries at different hospitals on the Internet.

Meet with the anesthesiologist, if possible, before being admitted to the hospital, discuss options for anesthesia – which, why, how and what to expect. A few patients are allergic to anesthesia and opt for hypnosis. Discuss this procedure in relation to surgery. It is another way to stay in control.

Follow any insurance requirements such as pre-admission certification or prior approvals. Make sure your insurance covers your surgery or hospital stay.

Be as fit as possible before surgery or hospital stay, just as an athlete before a strenuous game. The more fit, the better the healing. Avoid alcohol and get proper rest and nourishment. Figure out some way to keep your spirits up. The more you know about your problem, the better your self-esteem will be.

Get copies of any recent lab tests or X-rays and question new tests. Obtain previous tests from your physician's office to avoid wasted time and duplication at the hospital. Many lab tests are perfunctory and the hospital staff frequently fails to ask if you have already completed a test relevant to their needs. Also, inquire about the need for taking unnecessary tests. The response that "Your doctor ordered it" is not enough. We had a friend that was admitted for Bells Palsy and within 12 hours, he had been told to take two EKGs about three hours apart, a Heart-echo Sonogram test, blood tests, and a CAT Scan of the brain. A MRI for an additional brain scan was scheduled, but rejected by the patient after some struggle. All tests were negative. His wife diagnosed the problem before he got to the hospital. Incidentally, Bells Palsy rarely has anything to do with the heart. It is a virus of the VIIth (Facial) Cranial Nerve, which curves around and under the ear and extends to the effected side of the face. The VIIth Nerve includes the eye, facial muscles, and mouth. The doctor's action was a good example of defensive medicine, which is extremely costly to the patient!

THINGS YOU CAN DO TO GAIN CONTROL

File an advance directive, sometimes called a living will or health care proxy before being admitted. It informs the physician about the kinds of medical treatment you do or do not want in the event you are unable to communicate your wishes. The hospital should have forms and other details to help.

Before signing any hospital forms read them carefully or have a relative or friend read them for you. Do not sign anything authorizing the use of a substitute surgeon or anything else you do not understand. Stay in control. Remember that you are paying them (or your premiums and insurance is) – you are in charge.

Learn what medicines and doses you will be given for the surgery or hospital stay. Do your best to monitor the medications you are given during your stay. If they give you an excuse of why they can not tell you, ask for the head nurse or your physician. Do not let them make an object out of you because they are in a hurry. That is their problem. The above mentioned friend rejected a medicine because it gave him stomachaches, however, the head nurse insisted that it be taken because it was the "doctor's orders." He took the medicine and had to have additional medicine because of severe stomachache in the middle of the night! They quit giving him the medicine when they saw what it did to him. Obviously, his word was not enough!

Assign a relative or friend to be your "advocate" during your stay. This person can assist you with any problems or concerns during and following your stay when you are not feeling well. Be sure to pick an assertive person because you are dealing with a closed system that will see your friend's involvement as interference. For example, an elderly person, recovering from hip surgery was moved into a fourth room during a 10-day hospital stay. Confusion and stress was caused not only to her but also to friends, businesspersons, associates, and relatives. An added strain above the obvious discomfort of being moved around. She could have used an "advocate" if such a service had been offered.

Know when and how often to expect visits from your physician during your stay. Call your physician directly for urgent concerns. If you cannot get hold of your physician, contact someone in administration. Keep a log of attempts to contact your doctor and if this is a problem, maybe you need to look for another doctor that has time for and interest in his patients. The above mentioned Bell Palsy patient did not see his doctor once, following the emergency contact, in the one day he was in the hospital! He did see a specialist, which was extremely helpful.

Question your discharge if it is earlier or later than planned, or if it is not planned. Some times we are moved out or about in a hospital because of the need for a bed, which has very little to do with our treatment or hospital stay. The biggest problem is staying too long. Inquire about any undue time in the hospital. Some times a motel room would serve the same purpose. If you can, leave the hospital before new-day room rates begin, and request an itemized bill and take it home with you. You can review it when you feel better and obtain explanations of any items you do not understand. Studies have shown that involved patients who question surgical procedures and hospital stays, and who interact with their physicians, receive above-average care while hospitalized. These patients stay in control.

The worldwide health care crisis is forcing us to change the ways we treat the ill. The impact of managed health care and national insurance concerns may help to reduce some health care costs, but it is not clear that our Self-Direction regarding health will increase. It is increasingly clear that many aspects of traditional health care will continue to change in the next few years. Will any of it change for the better? Health care can be administered to Self-Directed patients as well as NonSelf-Directed patients. What makes the difference in outcomes is who is in control. Today we see that the lack of medical staff using the resources of the patient more constructively has allowed a new player on the field of health care. It is no longer just between the patient and the hospital. It now includes the so-called health care manager, a voice of a distant system who rarely has any medical relationship with either the patient or the doctor. This voice dictates much of the care process, usually over the telephone. Managed health care is separating us even farther from our doctor. It is important that we maintain some control over, not only the health care system, but also our personal health since we are also recognizing the extreme importance of mind-body interaction.

Learn about the use of imagery in healing. It is having a great impact today and will be more involved in our healing in the future. Remember that our body is the healer. We just need to learn how to maximize the healing process by understanding the control systems of our body. This requires Self-Direction or active involvement in our health. We are not objects for others to manipulate or manage, which we discuss in more detail in Chapter 7 on "School and Learning."

---

[28] Goffman, E. 1961. *Asylums.* New York: Doubleday and Company.

[29] Duff, R.S. and Hollingshead, A.B. 1968. *Sickness and Society*, New York: Harper & Row.

[30] This is a forced-normalized distribution by systematic sorting of test items using the dimension of "most like me" to "least like me."

[31] Deardorff, W.W. and Reeves, J.L. 1998. Making psychological preparation for surgery part of our practice: "Opportunity Knocks." *The Independent Practitioner*, Vol. 18, No. 2, pp. 86-89.

Chapter 7: School Versus Learning

Let us return to the idea of education as an excellent form of COE to deal with CFEs. Struggling to learn a new skill or sport? Learning and Experienced Control Theory make good partners. The relationship is simple. As a learner, we increase knowledge or skill (COE). This leads to a perceived control OI and OE over control FI and FE. These shifts of increased Self-Direction (COI combined with COE) and decreased NonSelf-Direction (CFI combined with CFE) components indicate increases in our learning. Therefore, the upward spiral of Self-Direction reflects achievement resulting in increased knowledge, self-esteem, ego strength, and positive self-regard.

To test the relationship between learning and Experienced Control Theory in a special environment, the senior author recorded his experience of control FI, OI, OE, and FE, while he took flying lessons. Learning to fly is learning to orient a machine in a spatial coordinate system – a three-dimensional environment. This is a more complex system than the two dimensional system of the LIFE PRESERVER discussed in Chapter 3, but it is more typical of real life. The CFIs are the engine, fuel, oil, etc. The COIs are the pilots controls over himself or herself. The COEs are the skill of the pilot and capabilities of the plane. The CFEs are environmental pressures or all those things that could cause your plane to malfunction. You could crash, run into storms, mountains, or other planes.

DWT took 37 flying lessons following ground school. This consisted of one flying lesson about every two weeks. All lessons were in the air; so the experienced control FE included the Cessna 150 single-engine, fixed-prop airplane, the weather, and the shortness of the landing strip (2200 feet), the instructor, and many other external factors. His COE was his new skill in flying, that is, using the instruments appropriately within the capacity of the airplane and level of his training. The pilot was controlled FI by his fears and anxieties of failing or having an accident, and he exercised considerable COI over these fears.

To avoid writing down scores that would reflect desired outcomes and, therefore, confounding the test scores, the student pilot tested himself over each of the four kinds of control in a random pattern, immediately following each flight. These scores were then instantly covered after the response was recorded and never seen again until the end of the 18 months training period. This way he was able to control for desired outcome effects and sequence effects by never knowing what scores he assigned to the four components from any previous flights.

To analyze the control scores, the 37 lessons were divided into 4 groups, the first 10, the second 10, the third 10, and the last 7. The greatest change in scores occurred early, between the first and second groups. At first, the pilot was primarily concerned with what was going on inside himself (CFI). By the second group of lessons, his interest in the environment (CFE) had caught up to his CFIs. By the third group, the CFEs had passed his internal concerns. In other words, the pressures became more outside the plane rather than inside the pilot.

Over the first group of lessons, however, his overall experience of control FE dropped while his experience of control OE increased. Skill began to overcome environmental pressures. After the second group of lessons, his sense of being controlled FI began to drop. Consequently, control OI declined consistently over all the lessons. It was not needed as much. This saves a lot of energy because the pilot becomes less concerned with holding himself together emotionally, as his sense of mastery OE increased. His enjoyment of the countryside and his sense of being able to control the flying machine surpassed his fears. Controls OI and OE (Self-Direction) increased only slightly over the 37 lessons, while NonSelf-Direction dropped significantly. However, the actual mastery of the skill of flying increased a great deal, part of which was learned in ground school. Consequently, the ratio of COI/CFI and COE/CFE increased steadily as the flying lessons progressed.

The pilot had learned the rudiments of flying from ground school and the actual learning to fly was 'hands on' to reduce the fear as much or more than to increase the knowledge. Getting flying knowledge in the "seat of the pants" was the primary concern. However, the awesome fear of causing an accident had to vanish at the same time – an important part of learning to fly!

Learning to fly, that is the 'hands on' part, is an ongoing reduction in perceived environmental threats[32] and not just an increase in flying skills. As indicated, most of the increase in knowledge about flying occurs in ground school and during the first few flying lessons.

Thereafter, the training that goes on is the application of that knowledge. The continued application of new knowledge, such as actual flying, does not increase perceived control OE appreciatively. The ground school knowledge is being applied. Increased knowledge frees the individual from having to spend energy establishing control OI. Sweating on a cold day and the 'white knuckle' grasp of the yoke takes its toll on energy.

In learning skills (COE), particularly when there is some perceived danger CFE, increasing COE is the most important factor. Learning to fly is a dangerous adventure. Learning to reduce pressure CFE is essential to make flying comfortable. A person who can not reduce the sense of control FE will quit, because this person can not get the CFI under control. Remember that an increasing CFI follows an increasing CFE. Having to succumb to fear causes a loss of judgment and clear thinking – fertile ground for tragic mistakes and 'pilot error.' Interpersonal stress during flying also affects judgement, which leads to other kinds of 'pilot error.'

WHAT TEACHERS CAN DO

Obviously, most learning takes place in less physically threatening environments. Learning in 'safe' environments also requires increasing feelings of control OE. Teachers designing lessons should consider how the student's experience of control OE could be strengthened. As with learning to fly, reducing learning fears CFI and CFE can be extremely important. We can all remember the anxiety (fear) from being called upon to recite in class or to answer a question we were not prepared for.

Conscientious teachers are sensitive to these anxieties and attempt to reduce CFEs. However, the reduction of only CFEs is not enough. The teacher must follow through by encouraging the student to develop his or her own COEs. The world 'out there' is not going to make a point of creating a comfortable place for us every time we are afraid. We have to learn to create our own comfort by learning to reduce CFEs appropriately. Our teaching colleges have not been robust in their teaching of teachers to handle these strategies with students. Much of the time it is a 'sink or swim' situation. The learner needs to be aware of and be able to see and understand the source of CFEs. That requires frequent opportunities for student responses about the learning process. The more we understand the four components of control the more capable we can deal with learning or violence from others or ourselves.

In most learning, progress is rapid at the beginning of the learning curve, as in the first four flying lessons. The learner is very aware that he or she is learning. Then, as in any learning curve, the pace slows, and progress becomes almost imperceptible after awhile. The teacher's job is to design ways to keep the learner aware of growth in his or her competence level and pace. That growth may be so gradual that the learner does not know it is going on unless they get appropriate responses.

Sometimes certain tests in the classroom help students make progress. Particularly, for those who are doing well. For the student who is not doing well, frequent testing only reinforces the notion that he or she is 'dumb' or unable to do better. Parents' rarely give positive responses about the child's small learning progress. It is usually in a form that does not explain the elements that make for success or failure. All too frequently, we believe the end is more important than the means or process in learning. In the worst scenario, learning as a family value, does not even exit. Some times, there are psychological blocks to learning such as being told you are 'dumb.' Consequently, there is no point in learning. This block has to be removed before learning can take place.

Teaching machines – with computer-based instruction – and programmed learning have the advantage of giving the learner immediate feedback. The student answers one question and then immediately finds out whether the answer is correct. If it is incorrect, the student instantly finds out what the correct answer is and thus the student is involved with the process of learning. This sequence is repeated through a lesson until all the content is learned. Furthermore, students proceed at their own pace, directing their learning and increasing feelings of control. Good-programmed learning is an experience of discovery without the sense of failure. It can proceed without the social context of teacher, parent, or peers increasing one's anxiety and interfering with learning. The student competes with self-established learning goals.

Learning should be enjoyed in its own right without the external rewards. Rewards are fine, but they should never be the raison d'être for learning. There are very few organized efforts in society to reward individuals' contributions that were generated for the simple pleasure of contributing. Universities have their 'publish or perish' and Federal grants pay huge sums of money for new programs of research or initiatives in education. How was knowledge generated before these rewards? Some children now make high grades because they receive money for their grades! Is this an appropriate way to increase motivation for learning and, therefore, COE? We think not. Learning for its own sake should be the goal. In some early animal learning studies, Psychologists thought that learning in Rhesus monkeys had to be reinforced with food as a reward. However, they later found that the monkey would learn the task, take the reinforcer (a raisin), and simply tuck it in his cheek without eating it. The monkey learned for the sake of mastering the task to develop competence! He did not need the raisin, which was later confirmed in subsequent studies.

Despite the advantages of programmed self-instruction, it comprises a small part of learning. We are social animals. Can you imagine being bonded to a teaching machine? Children especially want to relate gregariously with their peers. They seek responses from others of their own kind, not just from programmed texts or computers. The effective teacher is challenged to figure out ways for learners to experience control in the social context as well as learning knowledge or facts. A common form of failure to learn in the classroom is the child who becomes the class clown to get attention. Rewards are measured by how often the other students pay attention to him or her, rather than by what is learned. Handled incorrectly by the teacher, the clowning draws more attention from the other students and becomes more reinforcing than learning.

FEEDBACK AND CONTROL

Embarrassing or punishing the learner does not increase COE. In fact, it does just the reverse. It increases the feeling of CFE, sometimes

to the point of fight or flight. Most tests measure success or achievement. They are rarely used to provide personal feedback or to contribute to self-improvement. Some students respond to tests with intense study so they can proudly display all the COEs that they have acquired in a particular area. Some students feel so much anxiety CFI that they are unable to control OI, because the anxiety takes their complete attention and exhausts their energy. It needs to be recognized that some subject matter is simply more difficult for some individuals than for others, even though their IQs are the same. Learning languages is a good example and requires sensitivity on the teacher's part to recognize differences in innate aptitude, as well as intelligence. Physics is easy for some and difficult for others. Student aptitudes should be part of the teacher's knowledge about the child's successes or failures in different classes because intelligence is far from a perfect correlation with learning skills in different types of subject matter.

The sensitive teacher presents a test not as a threat CFE but as an opportunity to continue to reinforce the learning process. The test becomes a device to measure how far the student has progressed, what the student has mastered, and what the student should work on to achieve greater mastery in a given area. It is merely a measurement, not a whip. This understanding takes time and effort on the part of the teacher. They must work with the student to be certain that the process is understood and utilized to the pupil's advantage. Comments work best when immediately explained and a remedy provided that is suitable to each child, not just for the class. Large classes miss this point altogether.

PRAISE AND CONTROL

Most, but not all, individuals need encouragement to learn. The kind of assurance that children receive, from home or school, will help to determine how and what they learn. Some professionals argue that learning takes place in the womb, which may be true. Formal learning, as we understand it, begins at birth. From birth, children are not aware that they are limited in any way. They are aware of their dependence on adults, but they have a natural drive toward mastery and competence. They think that all they have to do is become adults and they can do anything! We often hear, "Please, Mom, I would rather do it myself," or "No, let me!" Given their real capacities, children start out with a lot of confidence. They learn their limitations through the nature of comments about their failure. "You have got to be taught to love and to hate," – and we might add, to want to learn.

Guidance into what they should and can do is very important. As adults, we tend to over protect (many times for our own needs and not the child's) and limit the child's interest in expanding and growing in both COI and COE. The other extreme is the caregiver that relies too much on the child's ability to learn and gives no guidance, and therefore, sets no standards or values. Over time, however, some children are constantly told that they are no good at a task, and they feel an increasing lack of ability to do anything well. Such children will always see what they cannot do rather than what they can. They will have very little belief in their own abilities and will not work up to their capacities. They may have lost so much confidence in themselves that they do not believe themselves capable of what they actually can do. They have no confidence in their abilities to achieve control OE, and they quit trying. Such children perceive greater control FE. Many times, they take on the role of the 'dumb one' in the family. Such behaviors lead to depression that directly pushes COE down, according to our research findings. We know of a particular case where the individual was actually referred to as the "dumb one" in the family. However, he decided to put himself through college to see if he was. He earned a Ph.D. and became well respected in his field.

Children experiencing CFEs for learning are too common. Our society has devised a school system that turn out people less competent, proportionate to their abilities, at 18 or 22 years of age than they were at five. We are all aware of the 'smart as a button' three- and four-year-olds that grow up confusing their elders by failing in school. They generally do well in other areas like informal sports, which may go unnoticed, since there are no rewards. Our studies of college students have consistently revealed very low control OE in school compared to other situations.

What passes for teaching in many American classrooms is really faultfinding and classroom management. Too often, teachers feel insecure in their abilities to handle difficult situations and lack the COEs in terms of handling classrooms, particularly when they are large. One of the authors was even asked by a teacher-friend to talk to her high school class and give her some pointers on how to control them, since she could not. Most teachers are not aware of their stimulus value as appraised by students and downplay their relationships to students. Rather, they are expressing their lack of experienced control OE in handling complex situations of human and group dynamics, which they know less about than they realize.

Teachers themselves are products of this very system, and as students, they endured the treatment they pass on to their students. However, do not think of teachers as the bad guys! They learn to do it, not just as teachers, but as children, as members of their families, community, marriages, and churches, and in all the other situations, we have discussed, including the school of which they are a part. Parents and administrators put up with such behavior from teachers because it is precisely what they experienced as students themselves. Nearly all of us are products of the same self-defeating, ever-repeating system. Teachers and schools who try to be innovative and deviate from known ways of teaching are regarded with suspicion.

Many individuals grow up with the expectation that education is distasteful because it is equated with hard work. Learning is its own reward. Many never learn that simple truism. Why? It is common to work with families in psychotherapy that do not value learning. Learning, as a value, is constantly put down in some family discussions. "Experience is what counts," they say, even if it is the same response to everything. Remember the phrase, 'If we only learn to use the hammer, every problem will be a nail.'

A psychologically healthy family is a learning family, which is also an open system. Only then will the control components be balanced properly. Most school systems approach closed systems. Furthermore, since the schoolyard shootings, they have become even more closed.

Because of the complexities involved in predicting which students will exhibit violent behavior, many school districts are closing up the system as tight as they can. The July/August 1999 issue of Psychology Today reports Heath High School of West Paducah, Kentucky authorized a $148,000 security plan following an incident where 14-year-old Michael Carneal killed three girls. The security plan requires that all individuals wear identification tags around their necks when on the school premises. Students must sign consent forms allowing school authorities to search backpacks and cars for weapons. Before entering school each morning, students must line up to have their bags searched. The school has hired a uniformed, armed security guard. School officials have obtained two-way radios for staff members to wear for communication during an attack in the event that a weapon(s) slip by their inspection. Each classroom now has emergency medical kits and disaster-instruction manuals. Heath's High School principal, Bill Bond, states that, the "Concept of security is always going to reduce freedom. That is a trade-off people have been dealing with since the beginning of time." Now, other schools are following Heath's lead. In January, 1999, the U.S. Department of Education reported that nearly 6,300 students were expelled in 1996-1997 school year for possessing firearms, which included handguns, rifles, and other weapons, such as bombs.

Yes! Schools are becoming even more closed since the schoolyard shootings. Classes are regimented, guarded, students searched in an atmosphere of suspicion that has become jaillike, which induces feelings of powerlessness and helplessness. This is clearly an example of increased CFE or control from the environment, which causes powerlessness and the desire to fight back. Clearly, something has to be done to alter this trend. Is closing the system even more than before the only solution available? We think not. Schools can be made to be more open to the communities they serve. Auditoriums, gymnasiums, meeting rooms, and even classrooms can be made available to the public. Schools do not have to feel or act like prisons to be safe!

At home, we experience similar problems. For example, parents practice the same behaviors as teachers. Pick a day when you are home with your child. Every time you say "No," "Don't," "Stop," "You can't," "You're too young," "Wait, I'll do it," or any similar put-down, mark a note pad. You will be astonished by the end of the day. Not only will you see how negative your teaching is, but also, you will have an opportunity to think about the amount of your misspent energy that goes into negative behavior. Negative reinforcement leads to avoidance, positive reinforcement leads to attraction. With negative reinforcement, we avoid appropriate power and control development and engage in situations where we have inadequate power and control and end up doing what is inappropriate, such as engaging in withdrawal and depressive behavior. The result is anger or violence, from which we do not escape. Generally, negative reinforcement only warns us to avoid the person who administered it, whether is was a teacher, parent, or a police official.

Parents, teachers, or whoever must learn to strengthen a child's sense of responsible or balanced mastery OE by giving praise and encouragement. The child is well aware of most of his or her failures. However, no matter how much a child needs praise and encouragement, it must be related to the child's performance. If the reinforcement is not related to the child's performance, the child will probably relate it to the one doing the reinforcing – the parent, teacher or anyone in charge. Consequently, negativism is more associated to how the child sees the person, than how he or she sees his or her performance. The result is not more COE for the child, but a great deal more COI and CFE (suppressors), and more likely, more CFI results. The child learns to disassociate with the one in charge when the reward does not fit the deed, rather than incorporate the inappropriate positive feedback. In addition, some children develop an erroneous sense of their abilities when they do incorporate the inappropriate feedback.

What children need is realistic assurance that he or she can get it right. An educational system devoted to this principle would persuade students that they are strong, able, worthy, desirable, and capable. When learning is successful, the student will see a system that is friendly, interesting, and within their power and control. Furthermore, such a system would eliminate many of the discipline/violent problems that increasingly plague our schools.

The formula is simple: Too much CFE leads to too much CFI or acting out. CFI always follows CFE and demands more COI, which takes additional energy and may or may not happen or even be available to the child, depending on the child's home training in the early years. Control OE is discouraged and circumvented in the process of too much CFE and the child does not develop appropriately in his or her educational pursuit. Very high CFI usually acts out directly on the environment, reflecting inadequate COI. If COE is high in the individual, the damage can be devastating. It is just different levels of rage and violence, depending on the mix of control components!

EXERT CFE OR TEACH COI?

In a self-defeating system, much of the teacher's energy is devoted to exerting control FE. Maintaining severe discipline distracts the teacher from developing confidence in their students. It becomes counter-productive. As we saw with parents and children, enforcing control FE on others deprives them of the ability to develop their control OI. Then, when long-term control FE is removed (as when the teacher looks away or leaves the room),[33] students hunt to see what mischief they can find. More productive is the teacher who can find ways to help students develop their control OI. Then, students are their own disciplinarians, allowing the teacher to devote more time to more fruitful tasks. The inability to help students is because the teacher has learned that he or she does not have the proper COEs for teaching. Parents, laws, administrators, and school boards have taken away the teacher's ability to function with enough COEs. In addition, this starts early in their learning process. We learn management techniques rather than care of our child, probably starting from techniques learned from our own baby sitter.

We recently visited a high school classroom in which the teacher exerted a minimal amount of discipline. She allowed the students to sit anywhere they wanted instead of arranging chairs in rows and requiring students to sit in alphabetical order. She allowed them to choose their own ways of learning whenever possible. She rewarded them for thinking through concepts and not just putting them nicely on paper. At no time did the teacher let on that anything a student said was stupid. In return, the students participated freely in discussions, were orderly and showed interest in their own education. This teacher had only minor discipline problems. Students who were hostile and belligerent in other classes, continually in trouble with their teachers and administrators, were quieter and more polite in her room. They all had resources for control OI and could use them in her classes, they were successful in that classroom, and the teacher was well liked.

In another school, where students are actively punished for talking while standing in the lunch line, discipline takes up much of the teachers' and administrators' energies. Hostility begets hostility. Hostility at school gets displaced at home. Hostility at home is displaced at school. Where does it stop? Now we see it in the community gangs and increased violence in the schools.

Rewards have a much greater impact than punishment. In our hurry and in our frustration as teachers, with administrative chores and as parents, with all their responsibilities, we forget to implement what we know about human behavior. We become more preoccupied with 'just getting through the day.' We know more than we practice.

LIFE-LONG LEARNING

Learning never stops unless we chose to stop learning. Need to learn a new skill at work? Interested in learning a new hobby or sport? Do we want to try to improve the skills we already have, like in the figure here? Increasing the ratios of control OI/FI and OE/FE is the key. Non-threatening comments, encouragement, and the time-honored traditions of visualizing success and practicing until we achieve it, help us do that. One of the author's mother learned to knit after her 65 birthday. She went on to win awards at state fairs. She learned to swim at 75, something she had been afraid to try all her life. A protected, encouraging and supportive environment made that possible. Mastery breeds more confidence. The greater the confidence, the greater the mastery. More confidence, more mastery – a positive spiral that, once started, continues to grow and grow.

It is important to understand that learning does not only take place in formal education such as schools. Many people learn from other sources, such as their jobs, friends, family, social and fraternal groups, television, magazines, and daily newspapers. What is important is to be open and willing to learn.

---

[32] Not unlike getting over the fear of flying.

[33] White, R.K. and Lippitt, R.O. 1960. *Autocracy and Democracy: An experimental inquiry*, New York: Harper & Brothers. The original study was by Lewin, K., Lippitt, R., and White, R. K. 1939. Patterns of aggressive behavior in experimentally created "social climates." *Journal of Social Psychology*, 10 271-299. (Abstract) Five groups of 10-year- children were placed successively under autocratic, democratic, and laissez-faire leadership. Hostility, aggression, and apathy were much more common while autocratic control was operating. These observations are interpreted in terms of tension, restricted space of free movement, rigidity of group structures, and style of living.

Chapter 8: Balancing Controls

GENERAL APPLICATIONS OF CONTROL THEORY

The earlier chapters have applied the Experienced Control Model to situations that occur in most people's lives. General applications of the Experienced Control Model help in solving problems regardless of the situation.

CRISES AND STRESS

Life can be viewed as a continuous process of encountering CFEs and reducing them. We can increase our control over the environment (CFEs) by increasing COE or by perceiving a CFE in such a way that it is no longer threatening. Maybe it is something out of reach and we decide we do not want it any more. Students entering college feel control FE from professors, upper class students, the dormitory system, and a variety of other sources. They may feel little control over these sources and may even doubt how much control they have over internal impulses. "When in doubt, be devout," is not always the answer. Some cry because it is the first time they are away from home. However, by the time the students' graduate, they have figured out the professors, become upper class students themselves, and moved out of or learned to endure the dorm. What once were threats CFE, later become familiar and understood and no longer pose a threat. This is a form of maturity, some times referred to as a 'learning experience.'

Many people attend colleges, find jobs, marry, and raise families. The next step is usually a challenge and presents more or less CFE. If we are happily married or engaged, dating may not seem like the greatest threat in our world. Starting to date, or re-entering the dating game later in life following a divorce, may seem like a real threat. The first date presents control FE from every aspect of the situation for most people. Divorced older individuals talk about the fears of dating because they feel a loss of trust of others. However, after dating, their thoughts lead to marriage. Dating is no longer threatening, but the commitment of marriage is, since they have already experienced a divorce, which they define as a failure, or at best, a terrible mistake.

Members of every culture, from primitive to advanced societies, feel stress and engage in violence and rage. People who hunt to feed their families worry about whether or not they will catch the needed prey. They are no different from those who worry that they will get the contract, the order, the raw materials, or what the stock market does, or whatever they need to accomplish their jobs. Our society, albeit life, seems to offer unlimited stress-producing situations of varying degrees. We acknowledge this when we talk about the "Fast pace of modern life" or "Getting with the nineties." Life is no faster now than it ever was; a minute still takes 60 seconds to complete, notwithstanding the "New York second." However, we may believe that we feel far more stress than the bushman stalking his prey. Why is that? We have more possibilities in the fast tract to choose from than any generation that preceded us. More has to be considered and weighed than previous generations. Buying a car is an example; there are more kinds of cars and there are more features to consider when buying a car. The combinations are endless and then there are the different places to buy cars where, seemingly, the same car can be purchased cheaper. This is one simple example of the complexity of today's world. However, various Consumer organizations and information groups can help us make these decisions, which can be found on the Internet. Yes, there are still only 60 seconds in every minute, but there are more things to do or more choices to choose from in the 60 seconds!

If we were to walk through a bushman's underbrush, we would find that our perceptions and tools for coping would have to change. Our society puts a premium on competition, and we frequently define success as winning, not just playing a good game. As many coaches are found of quoting, "Show me a good loser and I'll show you a loser."

As we experience more stressful life styles, we also have more options. The bushman had no choice; if he did not catch his prey, he, and his family, perhaps the entire village, would not eat. In contrast, we have to choose among occupations, places to make our homes, job offers, supermarkets, gas stations, banks, and shoe stores. We have to choose between products whose differences are minimal. Choices may make life interesting, but when too numerous, they can increase stress rather than provide greater opportunities because choices take up a lot more time.

The experience of stress takes the form of CFI that, in some cases caused by the perception of a threat CFE, a crisis or simply the demands of everyday life. Stress is felt from CFI or CFE. We may think to ourselves, "Maybe I can not survive this pain or environmental pressure. What if I do something stupid and embarrass myself? What if I can not make it, I'll just die?" Stress can also originate from too much control COI and COE, such as overly high expectations of one's abilities or skills.

Hostile CFEs surrounded the soldiers storming the beaches on D-Day in WWII. Their fatigue and fears were their CFIs. Their abilities to find ways to survive were COEs. These were the need to help their buddies find ways to reach their objectives when maps failed them. COIs were the drive to keep themselves under control and to keep going with the recognition that the goal was obtainable and worthy. More than anything else, their COEs were the ability and willingness to act appropriately, even without leadership, in time of need. This ability saved many soldiers' lives when comrades and officers were falling around them.

Obedience To Authority

Haney, Banks, and Zimbardo (1973)[34] studied interpersonal dynamics in a prison environment by designing a functional simulation of a prison in which 21 male undergraduates' role-played prisoners and guards. Psychological testing indicated that the students did not show any pathology. Students were randomly assigned to the role of 'prisoner' or 'prison guard' and neither received any specific training regarding their role. The reaction to the confinement situation and the interpersonal relationships that developed between the 'prisoner' and 'guard' were unexpectedly intense, realistic, and in some cases, pathologic. 'Prisoners' experienced a loss of personal identity and displayed passivity, dependency, depression and powerlessness. In contrast, the majority of the 'guards' experienced a marked loss of identity, gain in social power, control, status, and group identification. The two-week experiment was terminated after eight days due to the development of acute emotional disturbances in the 'prisoners.' One-third of the 'guards' was judged to have become more aggressive and dehumanizing than was expected. The earlier study by Milgram (1963)[35] showed that obedience could be total in such experiments, however, in the above experiment the guards' role was never defined!

It is obvious that the power of certain social situations can alter one's perceived role to the point of their becoming aggressive when that is not the actual character of the individual! These findings help us understand the complexity of human violence. It also shows us how such violence is linked to roles we assume as guards, guardians, health care providers, judges, police, parents, office bosses, politicians, members of wealthy families, and heads of state. The simple fact of having the authority or simply assigned a role changes our relationships to others to such an extent that we alter our perception of the limits of our power and control. It was obvious in the above experiment that the guards CFE decreased, their COE increased, in turn CFI increased, and COI decreased with the 'prisoners.' This is a bad combination, one seen in the military with recruits, and particularly, female recruits.

UNANTICIPATED CRISES

In his pioneering work with the victims of the disastrous Coconut Grove fire in Boston in 1944, E. Lindemann found that appropriate interventions during crises could forestall later serious consequences. From his work, an important distinction has been made between unanticipated crises and normal, anticipated ones. Anticipated crises are common life events that most of us expect to experience and for which we can prepare. These include marriage, retirement, vacations, holidays, timely gain, or loss of a family member, change in a spouse's work, beginning or ending school, or changing residences. Unanticipated crises are catastrophes such as fires, unexpected deaths, illnesses, and natural disasters. Unanticipated crises give rise to high CFEs because it pushes us into the unknown and plans have to be changed immediately. To reduce this type of crises and therefore the CFEs, we prepare ourselves for what might happen, such as a tornado, a sinking ship[36], a fire, a plane accident, etc. The Boy Scouts motto "Always be prepared" makes a lot of sense throughout life. Simply put, such preparation adds to our repertoire of coping mechanisms. High coping preparedness strategies generalize and help control situations that cannot be anticipated, and there will always be unanticipated crises.

GENERATIVITY

Erik Erikson[37] (1950), who extended Freud's theory of human development through adulthood, offers a third type of crisis. The "epigenetic growth crises," which is a transitional period preceding a stage of emotional growth. The epigenetic stage model bridges internal psychological forces and the social context. Each stage is defined according to age-specific crises, and each crisis is defined as the interaction of the self with others in a crisis-specific way, which later is referred to as Generativity, usually occurring in the fifties. Generativity is a sense of caring for the oncoming generation. To reach this stage of maturity, an individual goes through a crisis in which he or she is in danger of falling into self-absorption, concerned only for what affects him or her without regard for those who will follow. The healthy outcome is the sense of caring, not just for one's children and grandchildren, but also the children of the community, church, and political or social systems. Many people, who reach this stage of maturity become involved in politics, even run for office. Many develop commitments to organizations that rely on volunteers to provide community service. We are aware of an individual who, after years of unsuccessful attempts to regain custody of his brain-damaged child in another state, turned his energies toward helping other brain-damaged children. Not only did this help satisfy his need for Generativity and make up for the emotional toll of a long court battle, but it also provided a service and created a model for others. Our ability to feel this sense of caring is a powerful COE that brings with it different types of coping skills, personal security, and identity.

LEARNING TO HANDLE STRESS

Our society rewards individuals for accomplishment and condones outside agencies for being responsible for our children – frequently termed the atomistic[38] family structure. This results in many children having crises related to identity, homelessness, and abandonment and to adults being confused about their roles and frustrated in the face of their role in the commitment to rearing their children. It is not uncommon for children to get in touch with the State Social Services to complain about their parent's behavior just because they are mad at the parents. Frequently, the parents did nothing wrong. Such actions are very frustrating and costly to parents, and to the State agency.

As well as learning to cope with the demands of daily life, we need to learn to handle crises of all types. People's pre-stress behavior patterns influence their responses to any type of new crisis, but these patterns alone do not determine the outcome. Rather, the interaction between one's previously learned pattern of behavior and the new situation makes the difference. Some of us have learned to isolate a single stress factor from everything else in the environment, focus on it, and deal with it in a very specific manner. Those who have not developed this skill may experience stress CFE as general or vague, thereby limiting their ability to cope. In contrast, those who can zero in or focus on the stress CFE are capable of exerting focused COE to remedy a change. We can only cope with and alter that which we can identify. Attacking smoke never puts out the fire.

One of the best examples of focusing on the stimulus that presents a challenging CFE is watching a college basketball game during a free throw. As we discussed earlier, the supporters of the opposing team want the free thrower to miss the basket so they use distracters of every imaginable kind behind the backboard. The free thrower, however, must focus only on the basket and not see the context of distraction. The ability to exclude the 'background noise' determines how well he or she copes with the task. Thus, the free thrower significantly increases the COE and reduces the CFE in his or her experience.

In contrast, mothers frequently learn not to exclude the background distractions of young children underfoot because of their responsibility to care for them – making focusing on other daily tasks more difficult.

We have talked about the four components as sources of strain either on ourselves or on someone else. Each of these components has extremes. From this, we can organize the conditions under which we experience stress. First, there is too much or too little control CFI. Second there is too much or too little control COI. Third there is too much or too little control COE and fourth, there is too much or too little control CFE. Remember that the strength of the sources can vary from very low to very high. They can be short and intense or they can be long term but mild. For someone in prison, the CFE may be long term and intense. For a child that has to experience ten minutes of 'time out,' it may be short and mild, but seem very long. For a female being raped it may be short and intense, but the trauma may be experienced for years with moments of intensity such as flash backs or nightmares. Stress, measured by duration, intensity, and kind, wears many faces and effects each of us differentially, due to our experiences, beliefs systems, and our personality makeup. Being forearmed to deal with a vast array of stress is the best preparation of all.

Too Much Control From Within

If we feel too much control FI, our physical or emotional condition is getting the better of us. If your problem is physical, see a physician. If the physician says there is nothing wrong, see another one. If a second opinion tells you there is nothing wrong, consider the possibility that your physical symptom has emotional roots.

Impulses from within are some of the most difficult to deal with because they often express, for example, genuine physical needs such as hunger, desire for sex, physical symptoms of anxiety, anger and rage.[39] Controlling these impulses involves addressing them in ways that are appropriate for us. An overweight person or a person with diabetes must learn to satisfy hunger with foods that help, not hurt. Sexual desire can be appropriate for the successfully married but is less easily satisfied for others who link sex with control and power that results in rape. Anxiety of all kinds can be controlled by relaxation,

desensitization therapy, and in some cases, medication. Anxiety is to psychology what fever is to medicine. It simply means there in an underlying problem (CFI) that has to be dealt with, whether it is panic attacks from agoraphobia or flashbacks from some trauma.

Many people can learn to exert the self-discipline their circumstances require. Angry people find that support groups are needed to help them, such as anger management groups. Weight Watchers, Overeaters Anonymous, and Take Off Pounds Sensibly (TOPS), for example, can help teach appropriate responses to those who need to control their weight. Similarly, "twelve-step" programs such as Alcoholics Anonymous, Narcotic Anonymous, and Gamblers Anonymous alter internal impulses (addictions) with emotional roots (CFIs) that manifest themselves in physical behaviors. The high failure rates are not the fault of the program. It is the individual's inability or lack of readiness to exercise self-control, even with the guidance of the programs, since low COI is part of the basic problem.

Too little desire for sex with one's partner may signal a dysfunctional marriage, an attitude of fear about sex, a physical problem that needs attention, or simply a difference in a desire for sex by the partners. Programs and medication for enhancing sexual drive are available. One has only to look at the magazines (tabloids) at supermarket checkouts to be convinced that most people perceive themselves as having very inadequate sex lives, which is totally in error. Sex is like everything else, some people like it more than others. Some people confuse it with love, and it ends up taking the place of love. Some have psychological problems associated with it because of sexual abuse in childhood. Some think it is dirty and some think it is the answer to all things. Sex does not mean the same thing to all people, in spite of what Hollywood promotes!

The support programs do not work the same for everyone. Some find their answers in individual counseling or psychotherapy. Some people resist psychotherapy because they believe that an inability to solve their own emotional problem is a sign of weakness. Many years ago, people felt the same way about receiving physical help.

Receiving help is not a sign of weakness. Professional help is just as appropriate when the problem is emotional as when it is physical. The difference is that physical problems are seen as beyond the responsibility of the patient. We go to the doctor or the hospital. We put ourselves in someone else's care, that is, we become someone else's responsibility, and they make us well. Such things as a cast on a broken limb may even be seen as a badge of courage. If we break our leg skiing, we are still the envy of our friends because of being on a ski trip. Even falling off the roof trying to replace missing shingles, while maybe not so smart, still gets us sympathy and attention. We have even heard patients say they wished that they were in a car accident or something so they could get some attention from their family. Receiving help for emotional problems appears to run against the American 'group think' of self-reliance and independence. However, it actually means we have to identify the fact that we need help and must participate in the treatment process. No one can alter the problem for us, as is characteristic of medicine. You cannot take a pill to cure emotional problems, you have to actively change something 'with the help of' a psychotherapist. Responsibility is still with the client!

If the problem is inside, mental, all in our head, and cannot be controlled by medical or physical expertise, then one must assume responsibility for getting rid of the problem (or the source). Sometimes, it would be helpful if psychotherapy was seen as teaching. If that were the case, we could all go learn to solve our problems just as we go learn to build a house, design a dress, or boil water. Our friends and family would be proud of our learning accomplishments rather than 'embarrassed' by having to attend psychotherapy.

Too much CFI can be damaging, to ourselves, to people around us, and to the world, if we do not control it properly. Controlling it requires COI. Just think how history would have changed if Adolf Hitler had participated in individual or family psychotherapy as a child and learned to control his rage and hostility. Hitler and other dictators are examples of high CFIs that become so large that context no longer matters – and the "whole world is his stage." Such behavior also happens with rage, the enraged individual does not care who is in the environment.

Too Little Control Over Internal Impulses

Some forms of emotion can do harm to others and call for more control OI. Some of us teach ourselves to "take a time out" or "bite our tongues" instead of swatting our kids or screaming at our spouses. Others learn to cope better through psychotherapy or anger management groups. Groups offer the chance to observe others dealing with a problem effectively and the group provides a forum where the individual can practice effective responses. Psychotherapy helps explore internal impulses (CFIs) and self-control (COI) and the reasons for why they are not effective in our adaptation to others.

It is possible to have too much COI. We become so determined and rigid about things that we become inappropriate and destructive. We try to teach our children to stay out of trouble by refusing to talk about taboos. We refuse to do or say certain things for fear of giving a bad impression. We work so hard to try to show that we are good and in control of ourselves that we lose track of ourselves and send all the wrong messages. We keep ourselves from making the best of many situations or enjoying many of the events that come naturally and should be enjoyed. Families that refuse to allow a child to marry a certain person or disown the child may have too much COI operating. They are likely to find they have no relationship with their children or grandchildren. The people who find it necessary to control the decisions of the church committee, then leave the church because the group will not follow their choices, frequently think they are greater believers than the other church members. Their behavior is self-destructive for the very things they claim to be most important, rigid control of a particular attitude or position to the exclusion of reason.

Too Little Control Over the Environment

If we experience too little control OE, we feel inadequate dealing with the challenge that confronts us. When experiencing too much control CFE, we might first check out our COE feelings with an objective friend or colleague to see if the high CFE is due to a low COE. In other words, perceived high CFEs may be more a function of low COEs than an environmental pressure. Maybe we are just not competent for the job, rather than the job being too hard.

What causes feelings of inadequacy? Many children feel inadequate compared to adults, because adults are bigger and stronger and can do things without asking permission. As children become adults, they should lose these feelings of inferiority. Many times, they do not. Parents and teachers are often responsible, but not always. In one of our society's most common styles of parenting, parents feed their own egos by putting their children down through punishment and other means. We belittle them and make them feel small, clumsy, or just not good enough. Often, the parent's own parents had put them down, and they adopted this style – the only behavioral style to which they were exposed. Most of the time they are not aware of what they are doing, or that alternatives exist. Parents sometimes drive their children to excel or engage in activities, not of the child's choice, but to demonstrate their own control and enhancement. Similarly, teachers sometimes adopt an authoritarian/management style that makes students feel stupid and incompetent. Getting the message that we are inferior and dumb, both at home and at school can build into a strong message to the child that lasts for years or throughout the child's entire life span.[40]

Talk to a friend or colleague who can help you through some honest introspection and assess your parental or other capabilities objectively. Think of yourself as having capacities or potential abilities (COEs). Perhaps you can play the piano and have musical talent, a capacity that enables you to learn to play the guitar. You are good at woodworking, or some other skill, and, with your dexterity, patience, and attention to detail, you have the capacity to learn the skill to a high degree. You have many potential capacities to develop skills, more than you know and more than you will ever use or have time to develop. Evaluating your skills and estimating your capacities will give you a more objective view of your adequacy and define goals and, therefore, a meaning of life for you.

If you find that some skills are not as sharp as they should be, improve them. Perhaps your boss is asking you to write reports increasingly often, and you have never been proud of your writing skills. Take a business writing course or tutor yourself with a basic text. Perhaps you have a capacity but have not developed the skill you need. If your job involves some accounting tasks and you do not know a debit from a credit, take an introductory accounting class or fine a self-help program.

You can sharpen and learn interpersonal skills by contact with others. Many opportunities exist in local communities at little or no cost. Skills at public speaking come from being active in church groups, political, social, or service clubs. These all can help in getting along better with others. Personal contact provides us with feedback information about our behavior and progress that is important for continued growth. Do not overlook self-instructional materials, such as videotapes, computer programs, and books, available from the public library. They can provide an excellent beginning in opening up new interests and skills – the COEs.

If you find that your job or another important situation requires skill you do not possess and are unable to acquire, find a way to eliminate those requirements. We might ask for a reassignment, ask that the assignment be swapped for one for which you are skilled. Change jobs. No one has the capacity for every skill. If you use your interpersonal skills effectively your boss will understand and appreciate the honesty. Self-styled "supermen" and "superwomen" are doomed to feelings of inadequacy and frustration because they simply cannot do everything, no matter how hard they try. Do not become indispensable, because you will be. Interpersonal skills are the basic ingredient in any development of COEs.

Churchill and Hitler are people who exerted enormous control OE by "fueling" their control OE with energy CFI. Therefore, final words of advice in achieving control OE: take energy from the passions in your life. The salesperson with "fire in the belly" will make the sale. The cleric impassioned by faith will reach the congregation. The pianist inspired by a score will profoundly entertain.

Too much control over the environment can be hurtful to us, but even more so to the people around us. Over controlling, domineering and authoritarian behavior disrupts interpersonal relationships, alienates others, and isolates oneself. One spouse who is over controlling creates power struggles over every issue in the home or family. These create anger, frustration, and intimidation among family members and set the stage for long term dysfunction of all family members. Over controlling or too much COE accounts for the majority of marital disputes. Arthur Schopenhauer's (1788-1860) two porcupines characterize sensible interpersonal relations. The porcupines have to be close enough to share in each other's warmth, but far enough away that they do not injure each other with their quills.

Too Much Control From the Environment

If we experience too much control CFE, we feel much pressure from the world around us. This includes pressures from our job, school, marriage, parents, children, finances, weather, government, or from any other source – real or imagined. The lessons learned at Littleton Columbine High School were that security might supersede student's rights. Really? The kids will have to give up some of their individual rights. We always start security by building a wall. We do not examine ways of better understanding the individuals' involved. Increasing CFEs is not the only answer to everything. Screening students, in an unobtrusive way, is possible. It will take some creative thinking, but it will be better than striping the student of individual rights and simply building bigger locks or employing the answer to all things, 'build more prisons.' Let us examine this issue in the context of the Four-Factor Control model.

On a personal level, if you do not understand the pressure coming from an external source, talk to a friend or colleague. Make sure it is someone you trust to express an honest opinion, and who will not just mirror your perceptions, values, or fears. Be wary of friends who only say what we want to hear. Tell your friend what is bothering you and ask whether your perception of the source of pressure is accurate. If your friend does not think your perception is accurate, you are probably responding to pressure CFI and are unaware of it. You may have decided that your teen-aged son is on the verge of delinquency because he looks like one of the "tough kids" you disliked when you were his age. "Nonsense," says your friend. "I always spend a few minutes talking with him when he finishes mowing my lawn. He is fine. He seems to like school, and he is doing well. He really seems to like that new girl he met at school! Those clothes and hair are just the fashion now. It is nothing to worry about."

On the other hand, your friend may confirm your fear. Then, your task is to divide it into its component parts, and keep dividing it until you recognize one part as being primary or the focal determinant. Consider Lance, a fifth-grader, who "hated school." It was a real threat to him, and he had the report card to prove it. However, when he divided "school" into its component parts, he saw that he did not like his teacher. She would not let him disagree with her. He did not like English because he had been sick during some basic instruction and had never seemed to catch up to the class. He liked art and he liked arithmetic. What first seemed to be a huge, unsolvable problem as an assortment of pleasures and small solvable problems, turned out to be smaller than thought and Lance was able to relax and excel at art and arithmetic. He got some tutoring in English and made up what he had missed. His new positive approach helped him communicate more effectively with his teacher, who in turn responded better to him. Soon, he decided he "liked school" and was succeeding in every class.

Lance's focal determinant was his failure in the English class, and tutoring, rather than punishment, was one of several strategies he could use to gain control. He could have "knuckled down" and taught himself, possibly with self-instructional videos or computer-based lessons. He could have chosen to ignore this pressure and continue to fail English. As it was, he recognized that continuing to fail was not his best choice, and ultimately, he found a solution that worked for him.

Pressures from the environment belong to one of two categories, situational (those that arise in particular situations and are impersonal) and personal (those that involve particular people like group pressures). In addition, they can reflect two different levels, such as systems (e.g., hospital, school, government, or religious organizations) or they can be limited to an individual's immediate environment, such as a few other kids in school. In addition, they could be anywhere in between, but for simplicity sake, let us further examine these on a broader level. We have discussed the individual level, but what about the system level of control.

A modern day example is Communist Pol Pot and his seizing of power in Cambodia in 1975, as reported April 1998 in a news column by Jack Anderson and Jan Moller. Only hours after the Communists had seized power in Cambodia, the translated words of the new power went out over the Khmer Rouge communications. The exact orders were, "Eliminate all high-ranking military officials, government officials. Do this secretly. Also get provincial officers who owe the Communist Party a blood debt." Before it was over, the genocide that was launched with those instructions would claim nearly two million innocent lives, which included anyone who was too old, too educated, too wealthy, or spoke a foreign language. These individuals were brutally killed, or starved to death during the forced death marches. All of the books the Khmer Rouge could find were thrown in the Mekong River or burned. This was a total loss of control by the Cambodian citizens while faced with an overwhelming CFE from a political system.

The system became almost completely closed inside of a year after the Khmer Rouge seized power. Reports of the atrocities taking place were spotty and nearly impossible to verify. Pol Pot and his henchmen did a brutally efficient job of closing the system by effectively cutting off all communication with the outside world. For example, only nine nations were allowed to have embassies in the capital city of Phnom Penh, all of them were like-minded communist regimes. However, even those diplomats were restricted in how they conducted business.

Life – and death – was much worse for ordinary Cambodians. By the thousands, they were dragged out of their villages to be shot, stabbed, beaten to death, or bulldozed alive into mass graves. These difficult to imagine horrors became the Cambodian "killing fields" under Pol Pot, which included over 1.7 million Cambodians, a quarter of the population. For those who survived the purges, life consisted of long hours of forced labor followed by long hours of political indoctrination. Each person was given only a half of a tin can per day of rationed rice. Families were kept separated and a love affair could be a capital offense, although marriages were permitted! The system of control was almost total.

Twenty-three years following his massacre of Cambodia, Pol Pot had a rough final two weeks of life in the Cambodian jungle, according to Mona Charen, columnist, as reported in April of 1998. He had severe diarrhea, was hungry, lonely and fearful of dying! The result of his over controlling of his people? However, later reports in May 1999 indicated that Pol Pot was executed at 73, April 15, 1998, rather than dying of natural causes, according to Benson Samay, Ta Mok's lawyer. Ta Mok is the man who replaced Pol Pot in his bloody power struggle in 1997. These facts are still uncertain. Clearly a function of a closed system!

Additional examples of system power and control reaching the most horrifying levels of violence in recent history was during Lenin's Bolshevik takeover, Stalin's Cold War, Mao's Great Leap Forward, and Hitler's holocaust and there are many others. It is hard to believe that approximately 50 million people were killed in WWII because of Hilter's exorbitant need for power and control. The closed system of control is the most dreaded and one of the worst to combat, short of war against a nation. Examples are the Gulf War to combat the atrocities of Saddam Hussein, or the Yugoslavia War to combat the atrocities of

Slobodan Milosevic. These genocidal, blood drenched century landmarks have yet to point the way to a worldwide policy for assuring that such tragedies will not continue. Where is the guarantee to the six billion earth inhabitants that they will not have to endure such tragedies in their lifetime? Even diplomacy has not been close to a guarantee.

EXAMINING LARGER SYSTEMS OF CONTROL

An examination of the system effects of Control Theory is similar to examining the individual. There is an exception in that the control components pertain to various aspects of the system, rather than only the individual's perception of a situation or of a limited context.

JUDICIAL SYSTEM

An everyday example most of us have experienced is the judicial system. The prosecutor is one system and the defendant another that is governed by rules of law. The judge is another part of the system with separate rules. Then there is the jury and witnesses with their separate rules. These separate, but interlocking systems look menacing to the novice and leave the feeling of being powerless and with a loss of control. How can this perception be changed? The CFE is the total, formal judicial system that is strange and foreign to the average citizen. How do we reduce the effects of CFE?

Becoming familiar with the judicial system reduces the unexpected and provides techniques for dealing with all aspects of the system. Education (COE) is one of the best forms of control there is. Once the situation is understood, the threat is reduced. This, in turn, reduces the magnitude of CFI. Consequently, the need for high COI can be reduced saving a great deal of energy allowing the witness to focus more comfortably on the situational stimuli, such as the attorney questioning them. A well-known example is that attorneys first conduct cross-examinations by asking the witness about their credentials, secondly, if this gets a pass, they question their knowledge about the case being investigated. If this second stage gets a pass, then the attorney, in desperation, goes after the personality of the witness. It is at this point that the witness should recognize that they did fine – and should relax! Regardless of how much the attorney badgers the witness.

In the court system, the more we prepare our testimony the more power and control we have. The Cambodian and other national systems are a different story. The control had gone too far and there were no alternatives for reducing the CFE in the Cambodian situation. Knowledge of the circumstances came to the public too late. This is where the media is invaluable. Other nations did not intervene early on and the feeling by the citizens was one of complete powerlessness and angst.

The same problem existed allowing the holocaust and other genocidal crimes against humanity. Only war or a greater CFE could end any of them. Such problems must be identified early on and some effort should be exerted to alter their course. This is a foreign policy action and diplomatic concern, albeit frequently an overly soft and ineffectual voice. Is it possible for America and other countries to accept a Zero Violence policy? How could we carry it out? Look around the world today and try to identify where the next human perpetuated genocide is or will be. How do we stop the slaughter, rape, and hatred-fueled uprisings? What responsibilities does the world have in this regard? These gruesome incidents are not only historical, they are happening in our lifetime and will again in the future.

Take for example, what is happening in Kosovo. Yugoslav President Slobodan Milosevic, a 57-year-old Serbian, was indicted May 27, 1999 by the International Criminal Tribunal for the persecution and murder of more than 740,000 ethnic Albanians, which were forced from their Kosovo homeland by Serb forces. The numbers are expected to grow as more evidence is collected. This indictment is a first ever for a sitting head of state, however there have been 89 public indictments in the six years of the Criminal Tribunal. Only eight have been convicted at the time of this writing. This indictment means Slobodan Milosevic cannot travel to any UN nation because of the threat of arrest, even after the 78 days of bombing was suspended.

Political Systems

Political systems have a history of appearing in all shapes and sizes with differing goals all the way from benefiting the individual to benefiting the masses to benefiting only the dictator. They appear at many levels, national, state, and local, whether it is the city or county. Most political systems are ostensibly designed for the benefit of the masses. However, it is very hard for the individual to intervene and have input in most systems and to develop a sense of control (COE) about their government. As we have seen with some political systems, intervention is totally impossible in some countries, and ends costing many lives.

In America, it takes very large groups or highly organized groups to have a significant impact on a political system. For example, it takes large groups such as the AFL-CIO, NEA, NRA, AARP, Common Cause, PACs, and other consumer advocate groups to be effective. Not only has the United States Government reached such enormous proportions, but also sections of the Government have grown so large that some departments are over controlling of the public (CFE). An example is the Internal Revenue Service, which has evoked hostilities from citizens and many segments of society. They have lead to congressional hearings about their abusive and malicious conduct in dealing with individuals and businesses.

Loss of control OE at the local political level, from experiencing too much control FE, causes a decline in political participation and develops apathy from "sea to shinning sea" because "my vote or letters won't count anyway." The feelings held by many of the public spring from the perception that those employees and elected officials in bureaucracies can hide in the bureaucracy and impose authority on everyone else. We have all experienced trying to run down responsibility for something in government to no avail. It is easy to avoid blame and control the public from a position in a bureaucracy. It is a small wonder that over 50 percent of the population works for government institutions – they like the power and control which leads to their personal security. It is a form of control OE. We should take note that Russia had such a large political bureaucracy that fell from its own weight and lost most of its power and control in world affairs.

Passing laws (like making sausages) has become so complex in America that no one fully understands the law that results from such a contorted compromising maze. Nonetheless, the populace is still governed by these laws, with little or no control over them. Whatever we criticize about the media, it goes a long way in sorting these legislative actions out for us. It helps people become aware of some of the problems, although we do not always like the way the media goes about their job.

How do we enter the system with a sense of control OE? Vote, be a worker on any level. Write letters to editors; belong to political or civic organizations or causes. Get involved and be heard! You will be amazed at what you can influence and change nationally, which gives us a sense of control OE without significantly increasing our control FI.

---

[34] Haney, C., Banks, C. and Zimbardo, P. 1973. Interpersonal dynamics in a simulated prison. *International Journal of Criminology and Penology*. Feb. Vol. 1(1) 69-97.

[35] Milgram, S. 1963. Behavioral study of obedience, *J. of Abnormal and Social Psychology*, 67 371-378.

[36] A major disaster in the sinking of the Titanic in 1912 was, among many mistakes, the anticipation that it was "unsinkable." Consequently, no preparation or coping skills were available to the survivors to handle such an unanticipated crisis.

[37] Erikson, E. 1950. *Childhood and Society.* New York: W. W. Norton & Co., Inc.

[38] The atomistic orientation opposes the family unit or family system orientation. The atomistic philosophy leads to the children being linked to one agency or group, the father to another and the mother to still another. Family interaction is not fostered.

[39] In 1974, the California Supreme Court issued its landmark decision in the *Tarasoff v Board of Regents of the University of California* (529 P2d 553, 118 Cal. Rptr. 129) with the following opinion. "When a therapist determines or pursuant to the standard of his profession should determine, that his patient presents a serious danger of violence to another, he incurs an obligation to use reasonable care to protect the intended victim against such danger. The discharge of this duty may require the therapist to take one or more of various steps depending upon the nature of the case. Thus, it may call for him to warn the intended victim or others likely to apprise the intended victim of danger, to notify the police, or take whatever steps are reasonably necessary under the circumstances."

[40] Tiffany, D.W. and Tiffany, P.G. 1996a. Control across the life span: A Model for understanding *Self-Direction. Journal of Adult Development*, 3, 93-108.

Chapter 9: Focusing on Situations

Because people are involved in many control problems, the situational categories are some times hard to tell apart. When does a business deal stop and a friendship begins? When does a 'soccer mom' cease to be a parent and become a competitor at a soccer game with her child? Different situations are difficult to tell apart by some individuals in terms of their ability to deal with them. New problems that arise in situations that we normally handle well may alter our ability to handle the situations when it is modified. For example, you may have problems taking direction from your boss, now that budgets have been cut and sales quotas increased. You had no problems with your boss before these changes occurred. Your problems are linked to the change in the situation. On the other hand, if you have always had problems working with your boss, through good times and bad, those problems are personal, not situational-linked. They are associated with your interpersonal skills. Most of the time, people experience situations differently and therefore react to them differently.

We do not react to all situations the same. For example, if we examine the coping skills of 3608 nonpsychiatric subjects, ages 11 to 99, across eight situations we find the variance in situations as noted in Figure 12, which was significant [$F(7,25242)=122.66$; $p<.0001$.].

It is apparent from Figure 12 that, as a group across ages, we generally cope better in such situations as "Same Sex," in the "Community," or at "Home," than we do at "Work" or "School." This of course varies by individuals, but is the typical average response of large numbers of people.

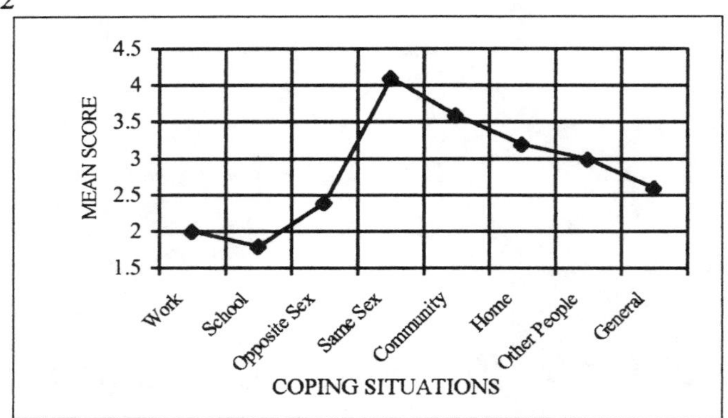

FIGURE 12. SITUATIONAL VARIABILITY IN COPING BEHAVIOR.

Some components of control are easier to change than others. This also depends on what kind of situation you are experiencing. Changing a situation can change the relationship between the people involved. If changing the situation is not possible, you can learn to ignore unpleasant aspects of the situation and emphasize the positive aspects. For instance, you might convince yourself that succeeding in the face of budget cuts and increased quotas are the kind of challenges that motivates you. You might manage people and resources differently, or creatively change some routine to be more efficient. The rewards, though not apparent today, will follow in time if you act on these new options.

A first step in solving personal problems is to ask ourselves whether the problem is our fault or caused by the situation. Look for patterns that can help you answer this question objectively. The point is not to assign blame. The point is to accept responsibility for one's acts and feelings and to learn to separate these personal characteristics from situational characteristics.

An example of personal rather than situational problems can be seen in the following couple. Nathan, whose third marriage is coming apart, and Sharon, fired from her fourth job in two years, should look inward to understand their personal conflicts that they bring to their respective situations. Problems within ourselves are the hardest to see and fix, but are the ones over which we have the most potential to control and change! Nathan and Sharon's self-examinations will be painful. They are in a position to "turn it around" by reducing excessive control FI, which in turn decreases the control FE for each other and on the job!

Is the problem really the other person's fault? Perhaps your mother really is trying to run your marriage and raise your kids. Maybe your boss really did cause you to lose a sale by interfering in the negotiations. Your best shot is discussing your feelings with the other person, reviewing the situation with the intent of seeking a solution and not casting blame! Your mother might have thought that she was "helping." Let her feel that you see her intervention as a constructive effort and you may help her to back away. Your boss may see new strength and skill in you, following your discussion, and have the confidence to let you do your job yourself.

Your last resort for dealing with control FE is to leave the situation. If your mother continues to interfere after you have done all you can, you may have to establish some rules, or you may even have to move farther away. If you have a bad marriage and have made a long and serious but unsuccessful effort to pull it together, your only remaining option is to end it. If you have a bad job, and have done all you can to improve conditions but still find it unbearable, you may have to resign. Such moves take a great deal of courage and may threaten your security, temporarily. Planning (COE) and patience (COI), before you take drastic steps, helps to reduce the risk. When the threat of CFE is more than can be endured, the *only* answer sometimes is to remove ourselves from the situation, which is also a form of control. We choose our environments all the time, but sometimes we feel that someone else is making the choice for us. Many Germans left their homeland under the Third Reich to find an environment less threatening. They lived.

What if leaving the environment is not an option. You may be an unhappily married Catholic who takes the churches stand against divorce seriously. You may be a child who would be better off in another kind of classroom in another school, but no other school is available. When changing the situation is not an option, you can fractionate the situation to accentuate the positive and minimize the negative. We develop better coping skills to deal with situations in which we find ourselves. The mother having trouble with a teenager will frequently fractionate the problem by saying, "He will grow out of it in time." In a bad marriage, we may want to 'accentuate the positive' by stressing the good things in the marriage and try to avoid the bad. This technique used to be applied years ago, but it appears harder to implement today. Today's younger population has a sense of entitlement in most everything they do, consequently, to be deprived of their wants is more of an insult than simply learning to do without.

Too Much Control Over Internal Impulses

Another condition arises from time to time, and that is too much control over internal impulses. If we experience too much COI, we feel blocked in our efforts to move ahead – to be creative and expressive and experience the emotions involved. We are confronting a problem, but we cannot figure out the solution. Most times, we know the solution; what we need is a way to put our solution into action.

Talking about the problem to a friend or writing about it in our journal often reveals the solution. Sigmund Freud referred to journaling as the 'magical writing pad,' for dumping the emotional 'garbage' we acquire throughout our life. When we communicate in speech or writing to others, we put the parts of our message in order so that another person can understand the message and not just our feelings. Journaling allows us to understand our own thoughts and feelings. Journaling is a process that is the same as analyzing the problem and identifying focal and contextual determinants, the first step in assessing strategies to deal with them. Sometimes, simply relaxing or "sleeping on" the problem loosens the controls we are exerting over ourselves and allows us to see steps toward solving the problem, that were suppressed before.

Solving Problems: The Process

Everyone has control problems. It is just different for each person. The problem is determining the magnitude of control relationships for each person for each situation. No matter what the source of a problem, the steps toward solving it are the same. First, identify the source of pressure, internal or external. Second, separate the pressure into its four control components and determine the primary focal determinant and context. Third, create strategies for addressing the focal determinant. One very good strategy includes talking the problem out with another involved person to reach a mutually satisfactory solution toward changing the focal or contextual determinants. Fourthly, if no alternative works, leave the situation causing the control problem. Some times, we face more control than we have the resources to deal with. Remember that it is generally easier to reduce many kinds of stress than it is to cure the common cold!

At first, reducing stress is essentially an intellectual process used to contain out-of-control emotions. It is guided by rational thinking, and requires learning to stay calm, as anyone knows who has tried to reason in the heat of anger. Those who do not identify the control determinants correctly, end up "kicking the dog" as a form of displaced anger. The kids may be sick, the washer may have flooded the laundry room, and your mother-in-law may have said something particularly cutting. However, when your spouse takes the brunt of your rage in a torrent of angry words, you are not accurately responding to what is bothering you. You are displacing your emotions on to others and not dealing with them. Consequently, they do not go away, you just repress them by displacing them, only to find they return later. In addition, you now have to deal with your spouse, on whom you dumped. An added form of stress! On and on and round and round it goes…

How do you know when you have identified the CFE that is bothering you and have chosen an effective solution? Again, because the process is an intellectual one, the right solution is one arrived at consciously. If you feel that you have been pushed into a decision by control FI or FE, think about the problem a little longer. Only when you feel you have consciously selected a carefully considered option, do you have the confidence that the decision is the best available alternative – the very best possible decision may not be available to you at that time.

Let us examine the case of Mike, who was painfully shy and feared public speaking (CFE). Mike needed tools to focalize with for dealing with control FE so he could fractionate aspects of it, but he did not know how to use these tools. He came to outpatient psychotherapy because he was appointed by the County Commission to head up a county fair. This meant a great deal to his business career and he could not let it pass. He accepted the appointment and then started to worry about the many public presentations he was expected to make.

The first thing we did in treatment was to evaluate the control he felt he lost in public speaking, which was found to be a great deal. Not only was CFE very high, but COE was low and CFI was extremely high in the form of anxiety during public speaking. He carefully made it through college without ever giving a talk in front of a class! This effort was by design. The next challenge of treatment was to help him focalize the loss of control in public speaking, which was associated to an earlier event in his life that was dreadfully embarrassing. This dreaded experience continued to linger on his mind. Consequently, we had to use imagery and progressive relaxation to quiet this earlier anxiety. He was reliving the experience each time he even thought about public speaking.

Focalizing became a matter of redirecting his attention to people he would be speaking to, which did not include any of the people in the audience from years before. He practiced focalizing on specific individuals, particularly his wife, to whom he talked daily. Once this was accomplished over several weeks, our attention turned to the topics to be presented. It was observed that the past embarrassment was an open-ended experience that was not well structured as to purpose or time. Therefore, Mike began to plan different talks, that is, fractionate topics for different purposes and with different content instead of being overly inclusive and wandering without knowing where to end. Although each talk was part of the whole he would eventually present, he limited his presentation to only parts of the whole and devised a personal purpose for each talk. He learned key words that would identify a specific talk with a specific theme that entailed a given outline and time limit. Each one was typed on a three-by-five inch card and he carried them every where he went.

By the time Mike made his first talk he was relatively relaxed and focused. His first talk was a little rough, but subsequent talks went very well. He remained focused and he fractionated each talk as he planned. He was quite proud of himself, pride he so rightly deserved. The memories of the CFEs were significantly reduced and the COEs had increased greatly. In addition, the CFI ceased to be a problem so he could relax the COI and redirect his energies to his talk.

CONTROL SCALES: STRUCTURE AND APPLICATION

The reason we use assessment instruments is the objectivity provided by measuring one individual against another. We need a standard ruler, against which we can measure acceptance or rejection of an individual's performance. We need an unbiased record to justify our actions when we make decisions about a person's personality. We need a record against which we can measure change in performance or behavior over time. Assessment instruments, when well constructed, are impartial and save time.

There are many other reasons for using assessment instruments in the screening process for job applicants. Presumably, we know what kinds of employees we want to hire and can look for specific profiles in the test results. Different job requirements demand different types of people who perform differently in different tasks. Some individuals meet the criteria for the job, but lack the personality to perform the job appropriately. Some individuals do not meet the criteria for the job but have a personality that is trainable for different jobs. Assessment not only helps us make accurate decisions, but also tells us the individual's level of competence for temporary jobs and therefore tells us the relative risk involved. In short, assessment helps avoid putting the round peg in the square hole. It reduces the turnover rate, costs in hiring, helps settle interpersonal disputes, and stress. It increases moral in the work place, cuts down on health care claims and sick-role behavior, and cuts down on absenteeism and tardiness. Obviously, standardized assessment, when properly administered by a qualified individual is capable of accomplishing many important things in industry.

All behaviors are based on control. Either you have control or you do not. The measure of control problems is fundamental to understanding all behaviors. The Tiffany Control Scales is a computerized or paper and pencil instrument for assessing many aspects of behavior. It selectively generates a report, three pages of data and/or 19 graphs for either a Standard Test or a Customized Test or both. The sections of the Tiffany Control Scales Standard report, which may be edited, include ten sections. These are General Information, Response Bias, Identification, Profile Type, Component Type, Coping Index, Level of Assertiveness Index, Environmental- vs. Self-Oriented Index, Commitment Index, and Chemical Dependency level. Each Profile Type, Component Type, the four indexes, and all sixteen personality variables are broken out by situations, which may be customized (demographics and situations) to meet organizational needs, and standardized by the user of the Tiffany Control Scales. The Coping Index provides a quick, reliable indicator of general adjustment. It ranges from powerlessness to authoritarianism. When evaluating an individual, the Tiffany Control Scales enables the Examiner to focus on special personality problems relating to specific control problems such as impulsiveness, lack of self-control, level of self confidence, pressures experienced, and others. In addition, the Tiffany Control Scales enables the Human Resource Director to more accurately screen applicants and/or fit them to specific types of jobs or evaluates them over time for promotion or reclassification.

For example, we analyzed a group of entry level employees according to seven Standard situations and ten customized situations. The high Assertive Standard items were Opposite Sex and Other People, and the high Assertive Custom items were Motivation and Avoiding Accidents. These findings suggest that the employees, as a whole, enjoyed being with other people especially the opposite sex and were highly motivated and would avoid accidents. The low Assertive Standard items were "Work," "Community," and "Home." The Low Custom items were "Inform on Peers" and "Training." It would appear that these employees do not put themselves out at "Work," "Home," or in the "Community." In addition, they do not aggressively pursue "Informing on Peers" or attending "Training' programs."

It was found that the high "Opposite Sex" average, a typical response pattern held by almost all subjects, suggested that there is common acceptance of being more assertive to the opposite sex individual. Being "At Work" suggests that there are many different reactions to that situation. In fact, the variance is so great that the second standard deviation runs from a minus six to a plus seven – a wide range for the norm of one situation. This finding implies that some people are very aggressive about being at work while others are very passive about it and probably do not care if they ever get to work. Obviously, one can be aggressive doing things, like "Being at Work," as well as with "Other People." Sometimes high assertiveness or even aggression is channeled into good things, like ambition.

Understanding control in the workplace is important since workplace violence, whether it involves harassment, threats, or a physical attack, is a serious and growing problem. Companies are being held liable for hiring violent employees or letting warning signs go unheeded. The lack of attention to the problem means lost lives, discontent and fear among employees, as well as tremendous costs to companies. In 1994, the American Management Association survey indicated that more than half of 311 companies indicated that at least one of their workers had been attacked, threatened or killed on the job over the past four years. The Labor Department research shows violence is now the number one cause of death on the job for women and the second for men, behind transportation accidents. One study indicated that on-the-job violence cost U.S. companies over $4.2 billion in 1992. Michael Mantell,[41] author of "Ticking Bombs, Defusing Violence in the Workplace," describes the profile of the employee likely to attack or kill in the work environment. According to Mantell, the violent person is a white male, about 35 years or older, sees injustice around him, has a history of aggression, poor self-esteem, and blames other people and things for his problems. In terms of the Tiffany Control Scales, this would mean he is impulsive with a high CFI, has low self-control (COI), and experiences high environmental pressures (CFE) without the skills (COE) for handling the perceived problem. All of these control characteristics could be measured upon job placement! Such an individual is Mark O. Barton, age 44. He was responsible for shooting and killing nine co-workers and injuring 13 others in two high-risk brokerage houses July 29, 1999 in Atlanta after losing $105,000 from his trading in recent weeks. He also had left notes at his home after killing his wife (two days earlier) and two children (one day earlier) with a hammer. He killed in the workplace to get revenge on those who had "greedily sought my destruction." When the police stopped his vehicle the same day of the office killings, he killed himself with a shot to the head. Obviously, companies must develop violent-prevention programs capable of screening and monitoring problem employees.

CONTROL THEORY APPLIED TO A VIOLENT CASE

One understanding of violence is the notion of the "Copycat." It is as though someone else did it, so 'why can't I do the same thing.' Dr. David Holmes[42] at the University of Kansas refers to the problem as "Behavioral Contagion." This behavior "occurs when (a) an individual wants to do something, (b) is restrained from doing it because society says that the behavior is wrong, (c) sees someone else do it and 'get away with it,' and then (d) thinks that he or she can do it also" (p. 199). He states that "A person has a need and they see someone else use a behavior that satisfies that need." The dynamic existed long before television or other media transmited such ideas. Holmes states that it is a well-established fact that publicity encourages copycat violence.

How do we understand the personality dynamics of a violent individual within the framework of the Experienced Control Model? To illustrate specifically, we examine the case of Kipland P. Kinkel within the Model and illustrate, using the Tiffany Control Scales, how the control components are involved. Let us examine his personality in general. He is inclined to be aggressive (his fetish for guns, torturing of animals, dropping rocks on cars, making threats, attacking a police officer, etc.). This would necessitate a high CFI and moderate COE, since both components are required to carry out an act of aggression. The proportions of the two components will vary in intensity for different situations. For the act to be violent, CFI will outweigh COI, indicating there is no self-control (values, responsibility, which is the incorporated CFE in early learning). In addition, COE is perceived to outweigh CFE – real or imagined. The relationship of these four components in Kip's case may be observed in the following diagram, Figure 13. The heavy outward directed arrows are the anger.

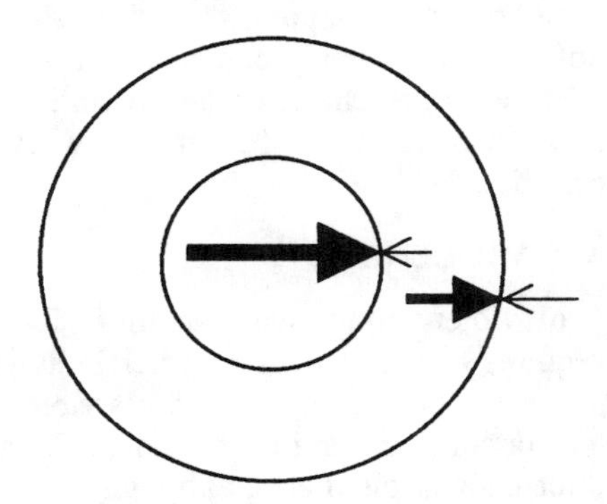

FIGURE 13. CONTROL DYNAMICS OF KIP P. KINKEL.

Figure 13 shows the heavy outward directed arrows of CFI plus COE channeling the anger toward defenseless students sitting in the cafeteria talking with friends before school started. The magnitude of the rage in Kip's CFI never can be measured during the time of the act for obvious reasons. The skill for carrying out this heinous crime depends on the knowledge (COE) he has of the guns used, his accuracy, his intelligence, and his cunning and preparation in carrying out a plan in terms of the school layout. The COI is usually developmentally weak or nonexistent in such cases. Whatever COI existed was rationalized away long before the school killings were committed.

We are defenseless most of our lives. We face many CFEs (terrorism, bullies, earthquakes, tornadoes, new jobs, hurricanes, wars, floods, unexpected events, etc.) because we rely on other peoples' COI (self-discipline, self-control, values responsibility) to keep their fears, anger, temper, and anxiety in check. In the case of natural causes, we have little choice but to be prepared.

Sometimes, CFE's are helpful and protective. The CFE that ended Kip's rage, as we stated earlier, was Jake Ryker's tackle of him when Jake recognized that the hammer of Kip's weapon struck an empty chamber. When Jake threw him to the floor, the CFE loomed much larger for Kip because he did not have the overpowering control provided by the guns. By the time a few more students piled on, the CFE was overwhelming to Kip to the point of subduing him until the police arrived. Obviously, it took a CFE to stop Kip since his COI was not able to control his rage. Consequently, greater CFEs (jails, police, powerful individuals) will have to be used to control Kip since his COI is unable to control his CFI rage. In brief, that is the purpose of prisons. Individuals like Kip over emphasized the perceived focal stimuli and lose sight of the other pressures of context, such as society's disdain for violence. Much of the contextual problem could have been resolved through school counselors, teachers, or family and friends. However, the narrow focus for Kip was to kill, no matter what the context. He saw only one alternative. Why?

VARIATIONS OF VIOLENCE

The majority of violent individuals are not violent all the time. Many times, it requires circumstances or other individuals to provoke their violence. That is why it is so hard to assess violence accurately by only testing the person and ignoring the situation. Situations frequently act as a stimulus for many violent acts, although we find exceptions in premeditated murder, stalking, and serial killing.

The nonveridical perception of situations may represent negative feelings transferred from a hated individual to one who looks or acts like the hated individual. It may simply be someone restraining another individual. It may represent a generalization of characteristics from a prior experience being displaced to a new experience. Our perceptions of others are rarely accurate – although we tend to think they are. We frequently have anger and we seek an outlet or release. Some release it in sports, ambition, talking it out, or just by keeping busy. If the individual is not able to drain off anger in these acceptable ways, then they make other individuals the recipients of their anger. Let us look at some examples. In the Appendix, we list 81 Component Types and some percentages of occurrences from a nonpsychiatric population and an outpatient psychiatric population.

Only five Component Types are presented here, which are taken from the 81 listed in the Appendix. These Types represent examples of the qualitatively different nature of extremely aggressive people.

#55 **DANGEROUS**: (High impulsiveness, low self-control, low competence, low perceived environmental control.) This configuration, as with the others, show high control FI (impulses). This is often the personality of a violent person. They most often show low self-control or self-discipline and rarely reflect great control OE unless the person is well experienced in violence, such as an assassin. Lastly, the perception of CFE is very important. If they regard the law with disdain and assume the law will not interfere, they will carry out acts of aggression far greater than one who fears civil incriminations. This person can be dangerous under many circumstances and situations. Some individuals with this profile will manifest severe emotional problems and may even display such symptoms as psychosis with hallucinations.

#57. **CAUTIOUSLY DANGEROUS**: (High impulsiveness, low self-control, low competence, and high perceived environmental control.) This individual is a lot like number #55, only the person is aware of the consequences of unlawful acts, and will do things to not be caught. #55 subjects do not worry about the law. The #57 individuals feel other-directed and do concern themselves with the law. They have a low self-esteem and are very resentful and devious. They commit violent acts where they cannot be seen and generally acts that started in other ways, such as rape, and ended up as murder because the victim resisted. Many rapists fall in this category.

#61. **VERY DANGEROUS AND POSSIBLY WHITE COLLAR**: (High impulsiveness, low self-control, high competence, and low perceived environmental control.) The person is very dangerous and does not fear the law. Such individuals are cleaver and will plan aggressive acts in contrast to number #55 and #57. Diane Zamora and David Graham would be a possible example. They experience a high energy level with low self-control or self-discipline and high control over environmental pressures.

#63. **MANIPULATIVELY AND DANGEROUS**: (High impulsiveness, low self-control, high competence, and high-perceived environmental control.) This individual is also very dangerous in the sense that he or she is very cleaver in planning violent acts and evading the law. They would have respect for what the law will do in response to their acts so they plan carefully. In spite of that they continue to be driven by impulse more than by a clear, articulated plan. Some of the schoolyard killings would fall in this category. They have high control struggles at the external locus. The self-control had not matured and probably never would in these individuals. Examples of adults would be exemplified by the murders of the Charles Manson group.

#81. **HIGH STRUNG, INTENSE, EXPLOITIVE, SKILLED IN MANY AREAS, AND CAUTIOUS**: (High impulsiveness, high self-control, high competence, high perceived environmental control.) This is the typical white-collar violent crime. They exhibit high drive, ambition, education, hold good or even professional positions, and carefully plan their violence. They are generally the hardest to catch. Ted Bundy would be one example. They have intense struggles at both the internal and external locus.

Even the examples of these five types depend on situations, size, and strength of the individual and accessibility of weapons, history of aggression, involvement, commitment and guidance of family and friends, and temptation or ease of committing the violence. Other component types are also described in the Appendix.

CAN WE MEASURE VIOLENCE?

We have evaluated many murderers in the past, but their personalities were evaluated only after they were apprehended and subdued by being in custody, usually under heavy guard. DWT evaluated a serial killer that was about five feet eight inches tall and had so many guards around him that they would not fit into the therapy office. It is impossible to assess violence at the time of the crime so assessment has to be accomplished earlier, such as in the school environment. We believe that the potential for individuals qualified to administer and interpret proper psychological instruments such as the Tiffany Control Scales can assess violence. Examining the responses to a Four-Factor Control Model, which is inextricably tied to situations, has not been publicly available to assess violence in the past.

Many murderers become very religious after incarceration. Measures of offenders in rages, at the time of the incident, can never be obtained. Our best efforts will have to come from instituting routine screening of personalities in grade school and high school. These measures must be designed to assess potential for loss of control and other problems before the crime is committed. This can be instituted as easily as measuring intelligence, aptitude, achievement, and performance at selected grade levels. In fact, a standardized test like the Tiffany Control Scales would take less time than many tests given now.

The enormous problem confronting society is "What should be done when the test findings show that the child could be a problem to self or society?" This problem has been dodged for years. Many violent individuals were known to be "different" in many ways. Some of the ways clearly pointed to violence such as torturing and killing animals, talking about killing others, etc. This seems to be a concern for the school psychologist and, subsequently, a conversation with the parents and a referral to a licensed mental health worker outside the school system would be in order. However, this does not happen because many school psychologists refer to themselves as 'step sisters' in the school system and do not have the resources or authority to voice such concerns. The concern of the school should be to identify, in a systematic and routine program, problems as early as possible. Once identified, definitive actions should be taken to enlighten the school administration, the family, and the child. A record of this action should be made and kept in the school psychologist's office for future reference, which should also indicate what actions were taken. Such a program will obviously cause some concern for school boards, however, they need to consider the alternatives such as the lives, property, and money saved in the long run. The school board discussion of this topic will cause considerable debate, which should be made public in the local media.

The current alternative to screening individuals in the school system is to incorporate metal detectors, use teachers' class behavioral reports, and for teachers' to be better trained to watch for deviant behaviors. The problem of watching for deviant behavior is that teachers' are part of the stimulus in the situation to the extent that some teachers have more problems with kids than do other teachers. We have known teachers that have asked therapists to attend their classes to help them understand how to control the acting-out kids. Unfortunately, this kind of openness on the part of teachers is rare.

What is normal behavior in the classroom? Whether good or bad, teachers have to manage children's behavior. No one individual has a handle on what is normal, but we do know what is acceptable behavior.

For example, for a sample of 1032 school children ages 11 to 17, based on the Tiffany Control Scales for the School situation, the mean level of assertiveness score is -.43 and the standard deviation is 3.54, which means that a score above 3.11 or below –3.97 would be considered a potential problem. A score above 6.65 or below -7.51 would suggest serious problems. The high score denotes aggression and the low score denotes passivity, which can also lead to temper outbursts. The upper range was 13.90 and the lower range was –14.00, indicating that there are a few children (about 40) who fall in the aggressive range and a few more (about 115) who fall in the passive range. The majority of children were in the normal range. Whether or not the 40 plus children would commit violence would depend on a number of other factors. These consist of the quality of their support system (family or friends), whether or not they had appropriate outlets (e.g., sports) for their aggression (CFI plus COE). These factors also depend on the degree of chronicity of their anger, and the amount of self-control (COI) they have learned and possess. To borrow an idea from Shakespeare, "'Tis the pattern of control and the situation wherein we will pique the conscience of aggressive acts."

It is easy to calculate which child is 'at risk' at school! The next stage is to examine the four control components to see which component is contributing most to the overall score. If it is CFI, we know a serious impulse problem exists. If it is a low COI then we know the child has a self-control problem. If it is the COE level then we have a different kind of problem, depending on how the individual executes aggression. If the child obtained a high CFE then we probably have a blaming problem or an overly querulous environment. Once these facts are known, the records of the child can be examined and a history of events indicating given patterns of behavior can be determined and evaluated. The integration of such information is a good start for dealing with the problem, which should be in the school records. We have seen the potential for teenage violence but with steadfast obstinacy, treatment was blocked by the parents. Although they had blocked such remedial actions as family psychotherapy, the child was still incarcerated, even while the parents denied all the way that he had any problems. What these parents were denying was there own part in their child's behavior. These obstacles will continue to exist until the stigma for psychological treatment is totally erased. Much of that stigma comes from the fear that "once a twisted molecule, always a twisted molecule," which is perpetuated by a few individuals, mostly in the medical field. The psychotherapy stigma is far less threatening now then it was 30 years ago, but there is still some work to do. We remember when we were children that people had similar feelings about the medical profession. A few continue to with those feelings to this day. The media can help eliminate this fear in both the psychological and medical professions.

Standardized tests, tied to situations, should be used to understand nonnormal, deviant behavior – for the same predictive reasons standardized tests are used to understand intelligence, achievement, aptitude, and other concerns.

HERE AND NOW: WHEN VIOLENCE IS THE CONSEQUENCE.

For years, we have recognized that criminals who commit violence frequently do not understand that there will be consequences for their behavior. To understand this, let us examine the temporal framework, in which we all live and operate. This temporal framework is divided into the 'here and now' versus the 'there and then.' 'Here and now' is the experience, emotions and cognitions of our lives at any moment in time without reference to our history or our future. 'There and then' is what we did in the past or plan to do in the future, such as setting goals. Violent individuals are impulsive and generally commit violent acts in the 'here and now' for immediate pleasure without regard for the future consequences. Our main point is, if we have no sense of a future, such as goal planning, then we have no sense of the consequences of our acts, and we are more likely to commit violence. If we disregard the consequences of an act and only live for the 'here and now' we are more likely to release impulses and therefore lose self-control, resulting in impulsive behavior that could lead to violence. Individuals who understand and anticipate consequences, consciously avoid losing self-control and develop better COI capability in the developmental process. Too many individuals grow up without experiencing training and understanding of the consequences for their acts. They never develop the sense that the future holds consequences – such as societal punishment! This point seems obvious to most individuals. However, it is elusive to individuals driven to 'act out' their aggression since they are unable to experience, understand, and deal with the emotions involved.

---

[41] Mantell, M. "Ticking Bombs, Defusing Violence in the Workplace," as reported by Lisa Genasci, Associated Press Business Writer, June 12, 1994.

[42] Holmes, D. 1991. Abnormal Psychology. New York: Harper-Collins.

Chapter 10: Caves to Outer Space

Our lives are full of contradictions. We are both controlling of and controlled by our environments. We have concerned ourselves with freedom and independence as far back as recorded history and undoubtedly before. How much do we really control our personal world and how much do we need to control it? Many of us seek far more control than we are willing to accept responsibly. We are like the four-year-old that decides he can find his friend's house alone only to succumb to fear when the busy street corner does not have the reassuring presence of Mom. When the first humans lived in caves, the CFIs and CFEs must have loomed very large. Life at that time was very NonSelf-Directed. COIs and COEs were in their infancy compared to what we experience today, which is what makes us more Self-Directed. However, the perceived relationship between Self-Direction and NonSelf-Direction was probably pretty close to what it is perceived today, although the Self-Direction lacked a lot of the sophistication of modern existence.

Humanity's first concern with control was to provide the family with food and shelter. Over the years, we have demonstrated a remarkable ability to adapt to environmental constraints. However, we constantly strive for control and spend much time and effort in ethical and philosophical thought about how much control is possible and/or desirable.

Although we have developed skills that have removed us from the immediate concern of searching for shelter in a cave and hunting for food, we continue to push our CFEs to broader expanses which drive us to explore outer space. Consequently, our COEs push us to develop advanced space technology. Nevertheless, control OE does not simply represent increased skills; it also means a reduction of past threats from the old CFE. However, new threats are discovered such as meteorites and space travel, which calls for greater COEs. Let us explain this idea with a simple example. With the advent of irrigation, drought is less of a threat from the environment than it has been previously. The control we experience over the environment (COE) results not only from the development of skills, but also from a change in how we perceive and understand the environment. This raises new threats and concerns about the preservation of planet earth. We could summarize all this by saying that the individual has an immense drive toward mastery and control OE because they are perceived as bringing freedom, comfort, and security. However, too much control brings other problems such as increased power and control FE, the relevant responsibility, and when threatened by loss of control, violence. There will always be CFEs beyond our control until we develop new COEs to deal with them. On and on it goes. The old cliché, 'The more you know, the more questions you raise,' tells it all.

Just as we have learned how to gain more control, we have created a world that is increasingly more complex and harder to control. Early scientists gained control over the environment by inventing the sundial, but in doing so, they created new controls over themselves. Who does not feel controlled by the environment when the alarm clock goes off reminding us of the cozy comfort of a warm bed? As great quantities of fresh water are depleted, the skills of irrigation may be returning us to draught, requiring the development of yet, newer skills. Are we gaining or losing the capacity for controlling our environment and ourselves? By understanding and using Control Theory, we can move closer to a meaningful answer in balancing power and control. Perhaps "necessity is the mother of invention," but the drive for control and mastery brings about that "necessity." When our power and control needs drove us to make propeller-driven planes go faster, we made them bigger and bigger until we reached the end of the power curve – Howard Hughes "Spruce Goose." The next stage demanded a new invention, greater power and control, which was the jet-propelled airplanes that now exceed thousands of miles per hour. What is next?

The basic need of man to seek freedom can be perverted into a fear of freedom. This has been observed in Erich Fromm's "Escape From Freedom." The quest has been used to seek freedom for all individuals, and to seek it for some individuals at the expense of others. As in ancient Athens, the ruling classes were able to maintain their own freedom by maintaining the strength of their society on the backs of slaves. As in the "rehabilitation" of entrepreneurs after the Communist takeover in China in 1949, those individuals who had become liberated themselves, were put into bondage by various political institutions. One person's control OE is another person's control FE!

Sometimes, placing restraints on individuals has been rationalized with prejudice, and based on inadequate research, such as the belief that blacks were genetically inferior. Human history demonstrates that such beliefs are not always long lasting, and the class, which comprises the masters today, may comprise the serfs tomorrow.

Let us look at social or political control on a personal level. Parents control their children, but as young adults, the child should be increasingly and systematically free from parental control. Husbands and wives find a variety of ways of controlling their spouse, sometimes for the good of both and of the marriage and sometimes for selfish gains that are harmful to all members of the family. As parents become elderly, control shifts to the children and the way the children, as parents, use their control over their children is likely to be the way the new parents learned it from their parents. If this pattern is too rigid, it could cause problems – child-rearing practices change!

What can we say about the conflict between controls which are NonSelf-Directed (CFI, CFE) and controls which are Self-Directed (COI, COE). While our options may be limited – we do have options. In fact, our control may be the option to place ourselves under the control of another. When flying commercially, unless we are the pilots, we place complete control of our lives in the hands of an unknown crew, which controls the plane. Statistically speaking, flying is the safest mode of transportation known. We have had far more friends and acquaintances lose their lives in car accidents than in plane crashes. Nonetheless, given the option, we would rather drive or sometimes take a train than fly. Why? When flying, we experience a total loss of control. When driving, we feel in control, more responsible for our own well being, although we know it is not as safe – but we feel safer! The experience of control is frequently the perception, not the fact.

Airlines have traditionally tried to distract passengers by serving drinks or allowing them to listen to music or view movies. What passengers need is some form of being in control of their flight, such as knowing more about weather, airspace, airplane structure, and flying. This can be achieved by having simple plug-in consoles at each chair with a recording explaining all of these subjects for the person who has a fear of flying. This would increase their control and reduce their fear. Psychological preparation for a flying fear is nothing more than learning to relax using imagery to place yourself in a more relaxing environment somewhere other than in the airplane. Learning this desensitization technique takes time. It is not available to everyone, and is not covered by health insurance.

We frequently talk about freedom as free will. A right we feel every human should have. We overlook the fact that free will is a subjective feeling – better called a sense of inner freedom – which depends on harmony and integration of one's personality. Psychologically healthy persons, who willingly choose a responsible course of action according to inner standards, experience this inner freedom. The experience of free will is determined by cause/effect situations in the world around us (our experiences as perceived), and by the world within us as we understand it. When our world is orderly and manageable, both inside and out, we are able to exercise control over ourselves and the environment. That is the way we like it because, 'mental health feels good.'

Have you ever tried to diet and been invited to dinner with friends and served a rich, substantial meal? You have a choice. Should you remain true to your diet or accept your friend's hospitality. Both elements of the choice are the effects of psychological causes. One is caused by your ideal image of the person you want physically to become. This ideal is itself the effect of countless influences going back into childhood. The other is caused by your ideal of appropriate social behavior. The answer is whether or not finishing off your friend's dinner (one meal does not a diet make or break), can you start back on your diet the next day or does one minor interruption break down your COI? Do you automatically give in to the CFIs and the CFEs and then hate yourself? If one meal is a big problem, then your self-control is very volatile, flimsy, and crashing is merely a matter of time. More work is called for to strengthen your COI.

There are other factors, which influence our decision. One is the degree of psychological hunger; the taste appeal of the specific food on our plate and the eating habits which we have developed over the years.

No matter what we finally decide, who can deny that the decision is the effect of long standing influences? Of concern, is whether we are conscious of the reason for making the decision? If we decide to achieve a target weight, we will have made a decision, which we would characterize as control over internal pressures (COI). Our choice and action will have shown control over the inner impulses (CFI). On the other hand, if we simply have a desire to eat the candied sweet potatoes without regard for our diet, control from internal pressures has won out. In either case, so long as we are aware of what we are doing and why we do it, we will experience control over the situation. We clearly made the choice and were not driven to make the choice. We may later regret our choice, but we were conscious of our decision. We were in charge. Not all control is comforting. Ask the President of these United States, or any CEO of a large company!

FREEDOM OR INDEPENDENCE

Many people think that the process of creating our own meaning implies independence or freedom, but that is not true. It implies only that our situation is a consequence of what we make it. The old adage, "You made your bed, now lie in it," has a clear meaning to the many generations that have handed it down. It says nothing about independence, but it says a great deal about controlling our own destiny.

In our search through the literature and psychological studies over thirty plus years, we have been impressed with the fact that people do not have the independence that they think they have. True meaning in life is not independence, as is so frequently thought. Examples are the teenager who thinks he would find life meaningful if he were only independent, or the employee, who thinks his life, would have meaning if he did not have to take orders from his boss. The idea of meaningfulness is closer to a life style. People who find a selected life style may be quite independent in some ways, but they may also be quite dependent in others. Good marriages are a system of independent-dependent negotiations that varies daily. **The meaning of life is not foreordained; it depends upon your choices and goals.**

Many people, doing what would generally be labeled as trivial things, see themselves as independent. Why? Because they chose to involve themselves in activities that present challenges, they can easily overcome. The big challenges, the ones where there is a risk of failure, they avoid. This constitutes the meaning they ascribe to themselves. Why do some people aspire to be president of a large corporation or of the United States, while others aspire to less? The choice was not inherent in the individuals; rather, it was a summation of several conscious acts over time. It was simply an exercise of choosing alternatives everyday and meeting the demands offered by the available alternatives as perceived. It is like setting a general goal and following the best path of stepping-stones. The closer you get, the more detailed and the more desirable the goal.

We have heard many of our client's say, "If I had known how difficult it was going to be, I would have chosen another career." These people feel themselves incapable of confronting the difficulties that their choices brought to them. Their feelings of incapacity, of helplessness, arise as a function of a low perceived COE. The feeling is not necessarily because of a high CFE. They would have said the same thing no matter what career they had chosen. It is paradoxical but true that they have never learned that how they feel about themselves determines how they feel about their jobs. They have never learned to obtain a balance of control in their careers or their lives. This happens to an extremely large number of us. Unfortunately, it results in a sense of powerlessness and fatalism, which becomes a life-style.

Fortunately – and unfortunately, as well – we never can anticipate all the problems that a particular course in life will have in store for us. There is always some gamble in our selection. We cannot control everything. We may have noticed that every time there is a breakthrough in science, there are more unknowns raised than answered. With the discovery of DNA, it became possible to contemplate genetic engineering. That has raised questions about both the technological question of "How" and the moral question of "Whether?" The same thing is true in our personal life. Every time we answer one of the questions life asks us, we find that there are more things left to answer. We never run out of CFEs, thus it becomes highly important to learn how to deal with all kinds of control from the environment by developing a wide range of COEs. Increasing our COEs allow us to cope with a wide range of activities, pressures, and influences. If our work becomes overbearing, we spend some time on our stamp collection, which is something that gives us a strong sense of COE. A frequent mistake people make is that they can reach a place in life where there are no more CFEs. The trick is to place yourself where you feel you can handle the CFEs that typify your environment. We have friends that regularly abandon their beautiful house with its city protection and convenience to live on an island in Canada for the summer. There they have to fend against bears, cope with outdoor toilets, and many other inconveniences. They choose their CFEs, at least for the summer, and they love it.

LIFE – A CONTINUOUS PROCESS OF BECOMING[43]

Life is a continuous process of facing one problem CFE, solving it through control over the environment, and then finding a new CFE confronting us. The skills that we developed to exercise control over the environment must continue to develop to keep up with the never-ending ripples of new frontiers – new experiences. The idea of the "last frontier" may be true in American history; but in the personal history of our own life, it is a myth. We face a kaleidoscopic array of ever becoming somebody else in terms of new coping skills – although the history lingers on. To repeat Karl Menninger's comment on his 85th birthday, "I feel like a young man with something wrong with him," says that there is always continuity of self. Even if there are new perceptions experienced as a functional person controlling our life. We may never know what is wrong with us (changed CFI), but it tells us there is something we should prepare for, with appropriate exercise, eating habits, and value development! Some sage comments that insure

Self-Direction are "Keep moving," and "Don't fall in love with your bed."

The give and take in the ever-changing configuration of the experienced control components will have a different meaning in every situation. Suppose the CFEs in your life were held constant by some outside power. You would still experience changes in your other experienced control components. However, suppose, for a second, that the kinds of control over the environment you bring to bear against the control from the environment were unalterable because of factors in your mental or physical endowment. The CFEs might not change. However, your perception of CFEs could reduce them to manageable fractions ("look at only the good things") so that your stress would be relaxed. Your environment would feel safer and more stable for you, although it had not changed at all. Meaning may be affected by what happens "out there," but in the final analysis, it still comes from within. Perceiving our environment in a more "positive" way can alter the meaning of stress from the environment even though nothing actually changed "out there." For example, in a study in a nursing home, it was found that the residents felt significantly more control over their lives simply because they were allowed to pick out the flowers they wanted for their rooms. How many stories have we heard of the physically challenged individual overcoming obstacles to participate in the sports they love, such as football, skiing, track, swimming, etc.

Knowledge of Control Theory can help you get more control over your personal life. However, like many other things, it will also raise questions. We have found how little control many people actually have in the real world. That is, real (physical) control, as opposed to experiencing controls. It is important to understand the distinction between control as we experience it, in contrast to understanding our life based on some form of physical control.

Control Theory explains how you experience control, and therefore how you feel about it and what you feel you can do with it. Nobody has complete control all the time. Indeed, in reality, you rarely have as much control as you like to think you have. That is why you should always be increasing the amount of control you have, however big or small the increase. Choose carefully which control you wish to change.

Unless you feel that you can control your environment, you will not be able to do so. The batter can never hit the ball if he stands there with his bat on his shoulder, unwilling to swing because if he swings, he may strike out. It should be remembered that a very respectable batting average in the big leagues is far below half the time's at bat. However, unless we swing, believing that we will hit, we have no chance to rise above .000. Obviously, risks are involved in trying to increase our experience of control.

We experience the degree and kind of control appropriate to our values and life style. We remember a couple, who bought a new house just like several houses on either side. We asked them "Why do you want a house identical to everyone else?" They answered. "We get to choose the paint." We could not help but think that they had chosen the degree of experienced control that they could handle without stress; and as far as they were concerned, they were in charge. We personally would feel that control over the choice of paint was too limited; we would want more choices, hence more freedom. However, for that couple at that time, they were facing up to what they thought were the real controls in their life.

---

[43] Allport, G.W. 1955. *Becoming: Basic considerations for a psychology_of personality*. New Haven: Yale University Press.

Chapter 11: Being Self-Directed

How Much Control Do We Have?

A common question is "How much control do we have over our lives?" From our years of research with thousands of individuals across many situations, we have discovered that the average individual, in the course of a lifetime, experiences about 12% more control over life than is experienced from life. Another way of saying this is that Self-Direction constitutes about 56 percent of what happens to us over a lifetime, on average. NonSelf-Direction constitutes about 44 percent of what happens to us over a lifetime, on average. The difference is 12 percent[44] in favor of Self-Directed behavior. The 12 percent control is only an average and can range from a minus 100 percent (totally NonSelf-Directed) to a plus 100 percent (totally Self-Directed). These extremes are highly unlikely. Someone scoring a minus 100 percent would probably be dead and a person scoring a plus 100 percent would probably be psychotic or in jail. The average difference of 12 percent will generally vary about 20 points either way over the course of one's lifetime, but the final average will still be about 12 for the average individual across many situations over a lifetime. Some time in our life we have all experienced the feeling of power as well as the feeling of powerlessness. It is clear which we prefer.

An individual that has achieved an enormous amount of control over himself and his environment, while as the same time experiencing an enormous amount of control from himself and his environment is Dr. Stephen Hawking. At age 57 he devotes much of his life to probing the space-time described by general relativity and the singularities where it breaks down. Much of his work has been presented on PBS Broadcasting. Most important to our thesis is that he has done most of this work while confined to a wheelchair and unable to speak due to a progressive neurological disease, amyotrophic lateral sclerosis, or Lou

Gehrig's Disease. Dr. Hawking is the Lucasian Professor of Mathematics at Cambridge, a post once held by Isaac Newton. In the late 1960s, Dr. Hawking proved that if general relativity is true and the universe is expanding, a singularity must have occurred at the birth of the universe. In 1974, he recognized a remarkable property of black holes, objects from which nothing was supposed to be able to escape. By taking into account quantum mechanics, he was able to show that black holes can radiate energy as particles are created in their vicinity. His international bestseller, "A Brief History of Time," spent over four years on the London Sunday Times bestseller list – the longest run for any book in history. Although confined to a wheelchair and unable to speak without a mechanical device he developed, Dr Hawking has shown a phenomenal grasp of the world and worlds around him with the greatest Self-Direction we have ever witnessed. He is the ultimate model and inspiration for the rest of us. He gives new meaning to the poem "Invictus," which we presented in the Introduction.

CHARACTERISTICS OF SELF-DIRECTION

The person who experiences an abundance of controls OI and OE is exhibiting Self-Directed behavior. On the other hand, the person who feels too much control FI and FE exhibits NonSelf-Directed behavior. Personal initiative and choice regulate Self-Directed behavior. The characteristics of Self-Directed behavior are self-actualizing, spontaneous, active, responsible, and creative. We control our own destiny. These are all characteristics, which we admire and respect in others, but frequently fail to develop. Let us look at these characteristics.

Different theorists describe and explain behavior differently, but Control Theory integrates many of these disparate approaches.[45] The concept of "self" is as old as American psychology. To be self-actualized means to be able to direct our behavior beyond those things that are necessary to their full potential. While each of us is an individual, each of us also has certain characteristics in common. One of the most important characteristics of "human nature," is gregariousness.

Man is a social animal, and hence the natural tendency of each person toward whom he or she is close is to be affiliative and cooperative. This is true, because we learn that lack of cooperation will result in poor or no social interactions, possibly leading to interpersonal problems and isolation, and perhaps even violence. On the other hand, while each of us has a social self, each of us also grows up into a social matrix in which we learn that it is necessary to earn the love we desire. We have conflicts, which will help us actualize our inborn selves, and some of those pressures will prevent these inborn proclivities from surfacing. For example, the oldest daughter who must remain at home, first to help care for the younger siblings and later to care for older parents, finds little opportunity to develop her potential in other areas. She has taken on the jobs of other family members as her own. She may exercise a great deal of control over this environment in highly specific situations, but other sources of her own development will be oppressed or very limited. The same is true of the middle aged parents of the "sandwich generation" who allow their grown children (some times with their children) to move back into the parents home. The parents find their adult children reverting to the way they were as teenagers and the parents lose all control and again experience much stress and grief.

Spontaneous As Opposed To Impulsiveness

We use the term spontaneous to describe behavior, which is self-initiated, not just a response to something. Spontaneous persons are not merely reacting to what goes on around them, but they are acting for themselves. When they act, they are conscious or mindful of making a choice among the options, which the situation has presented. We are simply being ourselves; we are in touch with our feelings in a rational and sensitive way. We are not being impulsive, but comfortable about what we do. We have worked out a good blend of CFI and COE working together to effect environmental change, which creates our expressions of work and play.

Self-Directed persons choose goals for themselves and go after them; they are active. They initiate plans and proposals to achieve their ends, and then they work toward bringing these plans and proposals into reality. They are realistic about what is useful and what is harmful in the obtainment of their goals.

Responsibility

Responsibility is a word that is often used very loosely. What we mean by a responsible choice is when the individual makes a choice for which he or she is prepared to accept the consequences. Every decision a person makes becomes a cause, which has further effects designed to not inflict intentional harm on others. Because no one can tell the future, no one can predict all the effects their actions will cause. Responsible persons accept the effects of their actions, even when they are undesirable and distasteful to them. They do not deny that they result from their actions, and they take whatever steps are within their power to rectify any damage they may unintentionally and inadvertently have caused. They own their actions.

CREATIVE

The meaning of the word creative should include people who are Self-Directed. Many people restrict the word creative to the arts. Poets and sculptures are seen as being "creative" and their practices are studied seriously. Cooking and sewing are practical activities, which on a day-to-day basis are not considered creative. The person who introduced cheese soufflé into Anglo-English culture is not identified and revered as is, for example, the person who introduced the sonnet (Sir Thomas Wyatt). While a beautiful quilt from the 1890's may be displayed in a museum, the statues of Rodin from the same period receive more veneration, and the identity of their creator is known. In contrast, the name of the quilt maker, equally creative in a different medium, is unlikely to be known. Both Rodin and the quilt maker were willing to listen to their own interior problem-solving mechanism, and reach for novelty in answers to the questions, which confronted them. They never settle for not finding workable solutions. The level of public veneration can never be known in most endeavors, we just do what works for us.

CONTROLLING OUR DESTINY

Controlling one's own destiny is what the Self-Directed person feels because he or she believes that what happens is in his or her own hands. We hear much rhetoric about our self-image but rarely do we take the initiative to do something about it. For example, we want to lose weight so we chastise ourselves every time we open the refrigerator door. In addition, doing so reinforces our poor self-image. We know that the average person asked to draw his or her image will draw it larger than it actually is. Try this exercise, get two long strips of butcher paper, and hang them side by side on your bedroom wall. On one strip draw an outline of yourself as you feel you look. Now stand against the other strip and have your spouse or friend draw your actual outline. Look at the difference. Chances are the outline, which you drew, is much larger than the one that is your actual outline.

Now that you know what you really look like, as compared to what you have been believing, think about what you are doing to the way you feel about yourself that causes you to gain weight (CFEs and CFIs). Forget about blaming yourself for eating too much. If you can actually learn what it is that you like or dislike about yourself (such as eating too much) you will allow yourself to make the changes that fit the actual image of yourself. You will find that the need to eat will take care of itself. In addition, from then on, when you make decisions about your weight, you run the show. You have become Self-Directed and have taken charge.

We must be aware that when we take charge there are certain factors which must be taken into account and which might upset ready made plans, such as one's health, the weather, social conditions, and the behavior of other people. Nevertheless, we must also remember that when Plan A is overturned by such a condition, we are capable of contriving Plan B to deal with the altered situation. Then no one will ever hear us say, "I can not do it this way," or "I can not do it that way, therefore, I can not do it." Rather we will say, "If I can not do that, I can do this."

Such, then, is the behavior Self-Directed, and the behavior of a person who experiences high control OI and OE. What about people who seem to be at the mercy of forces beyond their control? Machines are designed to behave in a certain way at all times. When we push the button, the buzzer rings; when we flip the switch, the light goes on. In the same way, the NonSelf-Directed person exhibits predictable behavior. There's a folk saying which describes such a person as one 'who takes a bath every Saturday night whether he needs it or not.' A caveat: Too much Self-Direction, like anything else, is a problem to others. Such an individual would be authoritarian and could be violent, depending on the balance of the four kinds of control.

CHARACTERISTICS OF NONSELF-DIRECTION

Reaction characterizes the behavior of the NonSelf-Directed person. Such a person waits until something happens, and then passively reacts to it. Some passively require someone else to structure their lives or to tell them what to do and to solve their problems. They merely go along with the ideas of others while contributing very little of themselves. Consequently, they have no control over their life and actually experience that they have no control and frequently resent others for controlling them! This response is typical of non-assertive people. Over time their resentment builds up and becomes either temper tantrums or passive-aggressive behavior. In more severe cases, the resentment becomes internalized anger leading to depression and suicide, or in some cases violent reactions. Hence, to escape from violence is through developing appropriate and balanced Self-Direction.

The NonSelf-Directed person is impulsive. Impulses are forms of control FI, but they are also frequently triggered by events CFE. First, the individual becomes aware of the event; then he or she emotionally reacts to it, unthinkingly; finally, his or her emotions suggest a reaction to the event, which is an irrational impulse. The NonSelf-Directed person does not screen these impulses but acts on them. He or she is often not aware of the connection at the time, and rarely stops to think about the consequences.

All of us have habits, and in fact, all of us need habits. If we did not develop habits, we would take much longer to perform such routine activities as getting ourselves groomed in the morning. ("Let's see, should I comb my hair before I brush my teeth or should I brush my teeth first?"). Alternatively, when driving ("Let me think what's the gear I have to have it in before I can back up?"). Nevertheless, the NonSelf-Directed person is at the mercy of his or her habits, now called addictions, to the extent that the person behaves habitually, even when it would be more rewarding and sensible to take some new pathway. Many times weight and smoking habits are addictions. Habits are easier to treat and change than weight and smoking problems that are masking some underlying severe emotional problem, such as addictions, like gambling, drug use or alcoholism.

NonSelf-Directed persons consider themselves helpless in the face of what happens to them and they constantly feel at the mercy of forces beyond their control. They are continually saying, "I could not help it." They feel they were forced to either act by an uncontrollable temptation (addiction) or their impulses "got out of hand." We frequently hear he or she "just snapped." Very young children may tell us that they did not do "it," their hand did "it." They have not yet learned that they control their hand. Some adolescents have a difficult time learning and accepting that we can and must control our behavior and take the responsibility for that control. We have all heard someone say one time or another "the devil made me do it." Flip Wilson made the phrase popular through his character Gerreldine. The reason we do not free ourselves is that the means of doing so never occurs to us. From this standpoint, the more conscious and mindful we become of our options, the freer we are and the more control we have.

The more we 'give in' to our inhibitions or repression of natural drives, which start in early childhood conditioning, the more we are pushed by forces over which we have no control. However, as we increase our self-awareness or consciousness of self, we simultaneously have greater control over our life, and experientially speaking, control over our life is the same as freedom. The reason for this increase in control is simply that the ways of achieving controls OI and OE are through our decision-making skills. The more decision-making potentials we are aware of, the more responses we have to control pressures exerted upon us, and thus the more possible it is to manage the controls FI and FE.

Many of the things we do extend from simple to complex stimulus-response behaviors. We respond to our childhood conditioning. We react from habit without stopping to understand if there was justification in our act. We must be aware of these determinants and then we can control this chain of events – bad or good. Now it is time to, **beat the system by programming your own life**!

---

[44] *Self-Direction* is 10 percent for psychiatric outpatient sample, which includes individuals who are in treatment for being too controlling of others.

[45] Tiffany, D.W., Shontz, F.C., and Woll, S. 1969. A Model of Control. *The Journal of General Psychology*, 81, 67-82.

Chapter 12: Captain Of Your Soul

THE MAN WHO WAS PUT IN A CAGE

What is generally referred to as "free will" in the literature is characterized by the determinants COI and COE in Control Theory. They are determinants, but they can be freely chosen. Perhaps this will become clearer by reference to Rollo May's parable of "The Man Who Was Put In A Cage," described within the experienced control framework. This parable shows the process by which control FI and FE were gradually reduced to automatic, NonSelf-Directed responses.

Once upon a time a king, bored, looked down from his balcony and saw an ordinary subject. "I wonder what would happen," he thought, "if a man were kept in a cage like the animals at the zoo?" Therefore, he put a man in a cage, thereby exerting on him control from the environment.

The man's first reaction was simply bewilderment; he had difficulty in understanding what had happened to him. He felt confused and anxious, which was a response CFI. Then he became angry at the injustice, which had befallen him. Again, a response CFI, but it had an important effect COE, for the man began to protest and complain in an attempt to change his situation. Often controls FI and OE work together in this fashion in different mixtures as an outward expression to effect change or damage on the environment.

Every day the king came to listen to the protests and to argue with the man, saying, "Look here, you get plenty of food, you have a good bed, and you do not have to work. We take good care of you, so why are you objecting?" The king was adding another form of control from the environment – an outside influence to the physical cage, which restrained the man CFE.

Gradually the hostility and rage reaction was delayed, as if the man was beginning to think that perhaps the king was actually right. The control from the environment, in this instance, was beginning to develop an internalized form of COI, with the help of the man's rationalization, which helped him repress his spontaneous rage.

Finally, the man found rationalization to justify his position. he argued that wisdom lay in accepting one's fate, and since his fate was to live in a cage, it was wise of him to accept it and enjoy it as best he could.

At this point in the narrative, we would like you to answer a question. Did the man freely elect to change his attitude toward what was happening to him, or did he change his attitude because he was forced to do so by circumstances? The man had an alternative; he could continue to be hostile until he died. Some do. Such an alternative results from an innate drive for freedom. The behavior he chose, however, was to cease (repress) his hostility (CFI). That alternative resulted from his circumstances from the environment. Both alternatives were causes; they were determined. Nevertheless, his choice between them was conscious. It was not "free," for if it were, it would mean that there was nothing compelling him in the situation at all; his choice was Self-Directed. From our standpoint, self-determination or the conscious, thoughtful choice between determined alternatives is simply the freedom we have in everyday life. The ability to choose consciously is very important to our mental health, and the more conscious we are of the choices we make, the better off we are. Our answer to the question raised at the beginning of this paragraph is that it would be "both." He elected to change his attitude and he was forced to change his attitude. Many of us experience this common situation in our lives. Perhaps not this harshly, but that depends on what happens to us as well as our experience of those events. Now let us go back and tell you the end of the story.

After the man decided to accept his fate, it was felt safe by the King to allow a group of visitors to look at him. The man talked with them very eloquently in an attempt to persuade them that he had really chosen his way of life and that they should adopt it too. He wanted, you see, to believe himself free, even when he was not. At last, he broke down, and instead of being able to speak connectedly, he would say, "It is fate," or finally and simply, "It is."

The man had gone insane from the terrible pain and hatred he was trying to repress. The combination of control OI and FE destroyed his energy, *viz.*, control FI and OE. This decision, unlike his earlier decisions to accept his fate, was not consciously chosen; this retreat into the labyrinths of his own mind was forced on him. Surely if he had done the choosing, he would have chosen to maintain his sanity. Nevertheless, the pressures were too great and the choices extremely limited. The repressive combination of control OI and FE acting against him forced him to reach the point where he could no longer remain himself and retain all that made him an individual – a human being. Something had been lost, something had been taken out of the universe in this experiment, and there was left only a void.

What was the something that had been lost? Freedom? No. In any absolute sense, the man had never had freedom to begin with. Can we talk about freedom for an ordinary person who has to get up at the same time every day, catch the same train at the same time to go to the same job? Then come back home at the same time to the same wife, watch the same television programs week after week, and go to bed at the same time? Regardless of how we perceive freedom for this person, there can be awareness, there can be consciousness, and there was choice. Although the man in the cage never "lost consciousness" in a sense, he became nonconscious. He did lose his consciousness of himself and his surroundings. Any time we let ourselves become pressured into an action that we have not consciously chosen and learn to adapt to something that runs against our grain, a good part of consciousness is lost to us.

Studies and common sense show that as control FE becomes increasingly dominant, there is a strong response from internal as an emotional or physiological experience, such as anger or an upset stomach or something else that drives us from inside. This surge of response from internal is an attempt to destroy the overpowering control FE.

The situation is complex. For instance, we can relinquish our sense of freedom in the present in order to obtain greater freedom later. We can, for instance, choose to attend college or a training school now so that we will earn more money later and thereby have a greater range of options open to us in future alternatives. Such a voluntary acceptance of control from the environment to obtain a college degree would not necessarily lead to the hatred described in May's parable. It was our choice and we know it is only temporary. In fact, we have institutionalized it by referring to such endeavors as, "No pain, no gain!"

Fractionating Control From The Environment

How do we avoid such negative responses from internal when we accept control from the environment? We do this by fractionating or dividing the control from the environment in such a way that we make only the positive aspects of external control the focal determinant. As pointed out earlier, in order to reduce the hijacking of airplanes, passengers must be thoroughly searched before they board their plane. At first, many individuals felt indignant because their privacy was being invaded. They experienced high control from the environment, and it resulted in a high response from internal. Later, the public outcry against such searches died down because the indignant individuals came to perceive the situation differently.

There were three elements in this change. The first was that no one felt embarrassed, because the same thing was happening to everyone and over time it became more accepted. Secondly, they began to realize that it did not represent a loss of their sense of freedom, but a gain. Because, if they were being hijacked on a plane they could not proceed freely to their destination; the searches were substantially reducing that potential loss of freedom. What they had originally experienced as being completely negative, therefore, they now perceive as something which had both negative and positive aspects. The negative aspects were greater control from the environment. The positive aspects were less control from the environment such as being hijacked. As we discussed earlier, the air travelers consciously separated or fractionated these two aspects, ignored the negative ones and focused on the positive. Third, in the course of focusing on the positive benefits, they also perceived the boarding inspection as a broader contextual determinant, rather than merely their own feeling that their privacy was invaded. The result of these three processes was that they saw control from the environment, originally perceived as an imposition, now as an advantage without feeling overly controlled.

Such fractionating of our perception of broader contextual determinants are common everyday experiences. Consider the parents of teen-age children. The adolescents can not seem to settle on any consistent behavior, and the parents feel that they must exert much control over them (CFE). If the parents could not fractionate the situation, their punishment might lead to such strong antagonism toward the children that the parents might tie them up, damage them physically, or ground them until they are 21.

We hear more and more cases of child abuse happening. These parents do not have the skills to fractionate the situation. Alternatively, if they were inhibited from directing their anger against their children, it might turn inward upon themselves, and they might wring their hands and moan, "Where have we gone wrong? Why have we failed?"

Most parents, however, deal with this situation by fractionating it and putting it into some broader contextual determinant. We say, "Oh, it's just a stage they're going through," and attribute the children's behavior to control from some internal pressure. On the other hand, we may say, "Oh, it's the gang they run around with," and attribute the children's behavior to some control (influence) from the environment. The result is that they do not blame the children or themselves, but feel that there are forces affecting the children beyond the control of either the parents or the child. Whether their perception is right or wrong, it provides the basis for motivating the parents to respond the way they do. The more informed the parent, the better the choices.

Such examples, as discussed above, show that the more conscious we are of our environment, and ourselves, the more decisions we can make to fractionate control coming from the environment. We set the forms of control from the environment into broader contextual determinants, and select and combine different methods of achieving control over the environment in dealing with control from the environment. Such broader self-consciousness results in greater openness and flexibility. The greater the openness and flexibility, in turn, leads to even greater self-consciousness. When Socrates said, "Know thyself," he put his finger on the primary cause of both good psychological adjustment and the greatest possible experience of human freedom.

We have the ability to learn how to control the magnitude of what we can bring to bear on COI and COE. However, it is also true that we can learn to select which elements of control FI or FE we wish to pay attention to and which ones we wish to ignore in order to achieve a more comfortable life. We can make the choice in a way that will bring us greater control and greater mental health. On the other hand, we can make it in such a way as to blot out of our consciousness significant elements of reality with which we should be aware. For selected periods, this can be good mental health. Over protracted periods, say months or years; it could lead to mental illness.

Even here the situation is more complex than it might seem. There is a choice within a choice within a choice. We may select to view reality accurately in certain situations and not in others. We may choose to ignore reality all the time, we may reach a point of not being able to recognize reality and thus become psychotic. However, if our boss says something to us which arouses our anger to a dangerous level, it would be more effective to exert control OE by either choosing to misinterpret what he said or ignoring it. Anything would be better than risking our job by calling him an S.O.B. On the other hand, if we were uncomfortable while flying, it would make sense to keep telling ourselves, "I'm almost there," even if we are not; it will make the flight a bit more bearable.

Everyone can supply further examples, for such simple ways of distorting reality are common to us all. Many times, they lead to good consequences. Many times, they lead to the "poor communication" about which everyone who functions in an organization complains. We try to believe the reality of the situation. Hence, when two people communicate, one of them may be talking about what really exists, while the other talks about his or her fantasy (perception) about it. On the other hand, they may both be talking about fantasies, but two different ones. This selective distortion of the environment is a form of a psychological pain reliever; but it is not without peril.

BEING DEPENDENT - WE CHOOSE!

Then where do we stand? Are we Self-Determined and capable of exercising control over our lives or NonSelf-determined and only tossed back and forth by fate? The answer is that we are both. However, we choose to be one, more than the other. How much control have we chosen to have over our life?

It occurs to us that we waited four months to learn whether our article is accepted for publication. Our bricklayers have changed the date three times before we can expect them to complete some work for which we contracted. The electricity rates went up 50 percent, a bond issue we supported was defeated, it has not rained for eight weeks, the stores in town didn't have a jacket the color we wanted, etc. This list could go on and on, and if we continued it we would start to get depressed. Many people, indeed, fall into depression because they have made only negative experiences their entire life.

On the positive side, our female boxer won a blue ribbon, we had another paper accepted for publication, found some old prints to add to our collection, and found the time to complete work on our house, etc. These kinds of experiences are also part of our lives. To which should we attend? How do we want to fractionate and concern ourselves with the happenings in our life? Ask yourself!

We have that choice – and so do you. Some items on both lists were capable of being affected by our Self-Determined actions; we supported the bond issue, which failed, and we wrote the papers. Others were less susceptible to our control. We have very little influence over the rain or the bricklayers; two elemental forces which no one can govern, and the blue ribbon was at least to some extent a function of the competition. Nevertheless, we do choose which type of experience we want, and herein lie the experiences of control – which is the experience of freedom. Some people erroneously attend only to what they cannot control; others, equally erroneously, only attend to what they can control. Remember that life is a continuous process of moving into deeper and deeper water. The complete mastery of the fundamentals presented here is your "LIFE PRESERVER"! The goal is an appropriate **balance** of the four controls, which will go a long way toward eliminating violence. Here are the tools, now the programs may begin!

Appendix

There are 81 different types of control combinations using the four control components in the following order CFI, COI, COE, and CFE. Percent of occurrence are given based on our sample (3609 nonpsychiatric subjects; bold percents = 603 psychiatric patients), if the percent is one or greater. The control components are divided into Low, Medium, and High. Finer divisions of the components would yield many more types. The types from the current division of Low, Medium, and High are as follows:

Component Types: (L = low, M = medium, and H = high)

1 (LLLL) Suggesting a low energy level and low Self-Direction. **(2.16)**

2 (LLLM) Suggesting a low energy level and low Self-Direction with recognition of some environmental pressures.

3 (LLLH) Suggesting a low energy level and low Self-Direction with the recognition of high environmental pressures.

4 (LLML) Suggesting a low energy level and some control over environmental pressures.

5 (LLMM) Suggesting a low energy level and appropriate control over environmental pressures.

6 (LLMH) Suggesting a low energy level and the experience of control from environmental pressures.

7 (LLHL) Suggesting a low energy level with high experience of control over environmental pressures.

8 (LLHM) Suggesting a low energy level with some experience of control over environmental pressures.

9 (LLHH) Suggesting a low energy level with control struggles at the external locus.

10 (LMLL) Suggesting a low energy level with over control of self and little involvement with the external locus.

11 (LMLM) Suggesting a low energy level with over control of self and some experience of control from the environment.

12 (LMLH) Suggesting a low energy level with over control of self and high experience of control from the environment.

13 (LMML) Suggesting a low energy level with over control of self and some control over the environment. (2.55) **(2.82)**

14 (LMMM) Suggesting a low energy level with over control of self and appropriate control over the environment. (2.41) **(2.16)**

15 (LMMH) Suggesting a low energy level with over control of self and some experience of control from the environment.

16 (LMHL) Suggesting a low energy level with self-control and high experience of control over environmental pressures. (2.05) **(1.16)**

17 (LMHM) Suggesting a low energy level with over control of self and some experience of control over environmental pressures.

18 (LMHH) Suggesting a low energy level with over control of self with control struggles at the external locus.

19 (LHLL) Suggesting a low energy level with too much self-control and with low involvement at the external locus.

20 (LHLM) Suggesting a low energy level with too much self-control and some loss of control at the external locus.

21 (LHLH) Suggesting a low energy level with high self-control and a loss of control at the external locus.

22 (LHML) Suggesting a low energy level with too much self-control and with control over external pressures.

23 (LHMM) Suggesting a low energy level with too much self-control and appropriate control at the external locus.

24 (LHMH) Suggesting a low energy level with too much self-control and some experience of control from the environment.

25 (LHHL) Suggesting a low energy level with too much self-control and high experience of control over environmental pressures. (4.71) **(4.31)**

26 (LHHM) Suggesting a low energy level with too much self-control and some experience of control over environmental pressures.

27 (LHHH) Suggesting a low energy level with too much self-control and with control struggles at the external locus.

28 (MLLL) Suggesting an appropriate energy level with low self-discipline and with low involvement at the external locus.

29 (MLLM) Suggesting a relatively low energy level with low self-discipline and some loss of control at the external locus. (4.35) **(6.63)**

30 (MLLH) Suggesting an appropriate energy level with low self-discipline and a high loss of control at the external locus. **(1.33)**

31 (MLML) Suggesting an appropriate energy level with low self-discipline and with control over external pressures.

32 (MLMM) Suggesting an appropriate energy level with low self-discipline and balanced control at the external locus. (6.43) **(9.95)**

33 (MLMH) Suggesting an appropriate energy level with low self-discipline and some experience of control from the environment.

34 (MLHL) Suggesting an appropriate energy level with low self-discipline and high experience of control over environmental pressures.

35 (MLHM) Suggesting an appropriate energy level with low self-discipline and some experience of control over environmental pressures.

36 (MLHH) Suggesting an appropriate energy level with low self-discipline and with control struggles at the external locus.

37 (MMLL) Suggesting an appropriate internal locus and low involvement at the external locus.

38 (MMLM) Suggesting an appropriate internal locus and with some loss of control at the external locus. (4.13) **(3.15)**

39 (MMLH) Suggesting an appropriate internal locus and a loss of control at the external locus. **(1.16)**

40 (MMML) Suggesting an appropriate internal locus and control over external pressures. (1.88) **(1.33)**

41 (MMMM) Suggesting an appropriate internal locus and balanced control at the external locus. This is considered normal. (35.80) **(27.20)**

42 (MMMH) Suggesting an appropriate internal locus and some experience of control from the environment. (4.32) **(5.64)**

43 (MMHL) Suggesting an appropriate internal locus and a high experience of control over environmental pressures.

44 (MMHM) Suggesting an appropriate internal locus and some experience of control over environmental pressures. (1.97) **(1.33)**

45 (MMHH) Suggesting an appropriate internal locus with control struggles at the external locus.

46 (MHLL) Suggesting over control at the internal locus and low involvement at the external locus.

47 (MHLM) Suggesting over control at the internal locus and some loss of control at the external locus.

48 (MHLH) Suggesting over control at the internal locus and a loss of control at the external locus.

49 (MHML) Suggesting over control at the internal locus and control over external pressures.

50 (MHMM) Suggesting over control at the internal locus and balanced control at the external locus. (1.91) **(1.49)**

51 (MHMH) Suggesting over control at the internal locus and some experience of control from the environment.

52 (MHHL) Suggesting over control at the internal locus and a high experience of control over environmental pressures.

53 (MHHM) Suggesting over control at the internal locus and some control over environmental pressures. (1.36) **(1.99)**

54 (MHHH) Suggesting over control at the internal locus and high control struggles at the external locus.

55 (HLLL) Suggesting a high energy level with low self-control or self-discipline and low involvement at the external locus.

56 (HLLM) Suggesting a high energy level with very low self-control or self-discipline and some loss of control at the external locus. **(1.16)**

57 (HLLH) Suggesting a high energy level with low self-control or self-discipline and a loss of control at the external locus. **(2.16)**

58 (HLML) Suggesting a high energy level with low self-control or self-discipline and control over external pressures.

59 (HLMM) Suggesting a high energy level with low self-control or self-discipline and balanced control at the external locus.

60 (HLMH) Suggesting a high energy level with low self-control or self-discipline and some experience of control from the environment.

61 (HLHL) Suggesting a high energy level with low self-control or self-discipline and high control over environmental pressures.

62 (HLHM) Suggesting a high energy level with low self-control or self-discipline and some control over environmental pressures.

63 (HLHH) Suggesting a high energy level with low self-control or self-discipline and high control struggles at the external locus.

64 (HMLL) Suggesting a high energy level with moderate self-control or self-discipline and low involvement at the external locus.

65 (HMLM) Suggesting a high energy level with only moderate self-control or self-discipline and some loss of control at the external locus.

66 (HMLH) Suggesting a high energy level with moderate self-control or self-discipline and a loss of control at the external locus.

67 (HMML) Suggesting a high energy level with moderate self-control or self-discipline and control over external pressures.

68 (HMMM) Suggesting a high energy level with moderate self-control or self-discipline and balanced control at the external locus. (3.77) **(3.32)**

69 (HMMH) Suggesting a high energy level with moderate self-control or self-discipline and some experience of control from the environment. (3.27) **(2.65)**

70 (HMHL) Suggesting a high energy level with moderate self-control or self-discipline and high control over environmental pressures.

71 (HMHM) Suggesting a high energy level with moderate self-control or self-discipline and some control over environmental pressures.

72 (HMHH) Suggesting a high energy level with moderate self-control or self-discipline and high control struggles at the external locus. **(1.11)**

73 (HHLL) Suggesting an intense struggle at the internal locus with little involvement at the external locus.

74 (HHLM) Suggesting an intense struggle at the internal locus and experiencing control from environmental pressures.

75 (HHLH) Suggesting an intense struggle at the internal locus and experiencing high control from environmental pressures.

76 (HHML) Suggesting an intense struggle at the internal locus and control at the external locus.

77 (HHMM) Suggesting an intense struggle at the internal locus, but an appropriate control balance at the external locus. **(1.16)**

78 (HHMH) Suggesting an intense struggle at the internal locus and a lack of sufficient control at the external locus.

79 (HHHL) Suggesting an intense struggle at the internal locus and over control at external environment.

80 (HHHM) Suggesting an intense struggle at the internal locus and much control at the external locus.

81 (HHHH) Suggesting intense struggles at the internal and external locus. (1.36) **(1.49)**

INDEX

G

H

I

J

Z